GENERALIZED

MICROECONOMICS

JIŘÍ HLAVÁČEK

MICHAL HLAVÁČEK

CHARLES UNIVERSITY IN PRAGUE
KAROLINUM PRESS 2013

Reviewed by: Prof. RNDr. Jan Pelikán, CSc.
            Prof. Ing. Milan Žák, CSc.

CATALOGUING-IN-PUBLICATION – NATIONAL LIBRARY OF THE CZECH
REPUBLIC

Hlaváček, Jiří
Generalized microeconomics / Jiří Hlaváček, Michal Hlaváček ; [English
translation by Simon Vollam]. – 1st English ed. – Prague : Karolinum Press,
2013
Published by: Charles University in Prague
ISBN 978-80-246-2024-4

330.101.542 * 519.86/.87
– microeconomics
– modeling and simulation
– monographs

330 – Economics [4]

CONTENTS

FOREWORD

This publication summarizes the results of more than ten years of theoretical research in the field of microeconomics at the Faculty of Social Sciences at Charles University in Prague. The objective of this research was to generalize microeconomics so as to enable modelling of economic rationality even in fields that standard microeconomics more or less avoids. These fields are not insignificant. For example, roughly half the financial transactions in a modern economy (including donor activities) involve redistribution. The profit maximization assumption makes it impossible to gain a microeconomic modelling insight into centrally planned economies and above all into the non-profit sectors of market economies. The same can be said for externalities (both positive and negative).

In our view, abandoning the *homo economicus* paradigm—in the sense of replacing it with a different paradigm with a different (alternative) agent criterion function that conflicts with profit maximization—is an impassable route and one that bypasses the treasure trove of knowledge of standard economics.

We have opted for a different path: we try to broaden the scope of microeconomics in order to capture the activity of non-profit institutions while treating standard profit/utility maximization as a special case. In other words, instead of abandoning the *homo economicus* paradigm, we generalize it. This generalization complements rather than challenges standard microeconomics. Where the *homo economicus* modelling approach can reasonably be applied, we do not feel the need to abandon it. We venture beyond the boundaries of this standard microeconomic paradigm primarily where non-profit institutions operate and where, simultaneously, economic activity can be both rational and irrational.

For us, the generalizing criterion is "Darwinian" maximization of the probability of survival. This criterion is not necessarily considered explicitly by individual agents in their everyday decision-making, but if they do not respect it they will not survive in the long run.

1.

THE GENERALIZED PRINCIPLE
OF ECONOMIC RATIONALITY

The decision-optimization principle contained in the *homo economicus* paradigm conceals an assumed preference for a situation lying on the very boundary of the set of feasible solutions. Unless a *homo economicus* agent (a model producer or a model consumer) can estimate how the parameters of his decision-making problem are going to evolve, he will opt for a situation lying on the boundary of his production or consumption possibilities.

This is perhaps one of the most contentious aspects of neoclassical microeconomics, since producers, for example, will in reality tend to have a legitimate distrust of, or even aversion to, extreme situations located at the limits of technological or financial feasibility and will therefore prefer production situations that lie inside the set of feasible solutions. Being at the boundary is risky, as even a small change in the parameters of a decision-making problem can generate technological inconsistency.

An even stronger preference for a solution that is an internal point of the set of feasible solutions can be assumed in the case of legal constraints. Balancing on the boundary of legal admissibility usually entails a lot of extra non-productive effort and costs. This applies most of all to small firms, which cannot afford expensive lawyers.

The decision-taker also has to ensure that his behaviour is understood by others and does not disrespect established practices. Here again, maximization of profit (personal gain) in accordance with the *homo economicus* model behaviour leads inevitably to situations lying on the boundary of social and moral admissibility, situations where cooperation collapses, social relations become chaotic, and conflicts and disputes break out with such frequency that resolving them can hardly be described as efficient expenditure of human energy and other scarce resources.

In our view, the standard *homo economicus* economic paradigm does not offer enough scope to cover all the ways in which economic agents behave. In line with Sen, we cannot accept the economic behaviour described by the *homo economicus* paradigm as a requirement for rationality of economic agents.[1]

Efforts to cover a wider context than the purely liberal neoclassical paradigm are not new, of course. In the next section we mention (briefly and without aiming to be comprehensive) some of the trends in economic theory in this sense.

1.1 ALTERNATIVES TO THE HOMO ECONOMICUS PARADIGM

We have already discussed the standard decision-making principle used in neoclassical microeconomics, according to which an agent chooses—rationally and perfectly—the option with the highest subjective utility from the set of feasible decisions available and is capable of implementing that decision.

One alternative to this standard decision-making principle is the satisfaction principle, also known as the bounded rationality principle,[2] which assumes that agents do not seek the optimal option forever: the search process is terminated as soon as a satisfactory solution has been found.

Another alternative to the standard decision-making principle is the concept of cognitive dissonance in an individual's rationality. This assumes that agents' rationality fails and that some agents systematically introduce errors, mistakes and distortions into their decision-making processes when considering past experience.[3] Cognitive bounding of rationality therefore essentially represents the consequences of human flaws (such as procrastination).

Another alternative to the standard decision-making principle is the concept of "hard-core" altruism, where an agent incorporates the utility of other agents, or other members of society, into his decision-making motives.[4]

There is also a series of model modifications of the neoclassical paradigm within the framework of the standard decision-making principle. Perhaps the best known is the labour-managed firm (LMF) for cooperatives, in which the

1   Sen, A.: *On Ethics and Economics*. Oxford: Blackwell, 1987, p. 16.
2   Simon, H. A.: Theories of Bounded Rationality. In *Decision and Organisation*, edited by C. B. McGuire, R. Radner, 161–76. Amsterdam: North Holland, 1972.
3   Akerlof, G. A.: Procrastination and Obedience. *American Economic Review* 81, 2(1991): 1–19.
4   A review of these concepts can be found in Hlaváček, J. et al.: *Mikroekonomie sounáležitosti se společenstvím*. Praha: Karolinum, 1999.

same group of people plays the role of both owners and employees. This model assumes that an LMF maximizes income per capita, where income is the sum of wages and personal income stemming from profit.[5]

Another way to extend the calculation of profit within the standard decision-making principle is to take into account the extent and magnitude of the effort exerted by managers.[6]

A further approach that does not involve abandoning the standard decision-making principle is the superintendent criterion constructed by Benjamin Ward in an attempt to describe the socialist planned economy.[7] The same can be said for the "*homo se assecurans*" model, where the producer's maximization criterion is the margin between its ability to produce and the output it actually produces. Chapter 6 of this book will be devoted to this model. The "employee escape" model represents another attempt to model and describe a centrally planned economy with typical excess demand in the labour market.[8]

The application of game theory, which takes into account the active existence of other economic agents and the predictable effects of their decisions on the firm's decisions, can also be regarded as an example of generalization within the standard decision-making principle. The same goes for models describing agents' efforts to acquire positional goods, or social status.[9] Buchanan's concept of club goods is also a generalization of the standard economic paradigm.[10]

Even the concept we present in this book, in which we try to construct a general model of economic behaviour, does not abandon the standard decision-making principle. As in mainstream economic theory, we assume that a decision-taker (economic agent) prefers (explicitly or implicitly through his decision) the economic action that he considers to be the best from his perspective, and has information on the consequences of all the possible feasible decisions.

5   See Vanek, J.: *The General Theory of Labor-Managed Market Economies*. Ithaca: Cornell University Press, 1970.

6   See Hunter, H.: Optimal Tautness in Development Planning. *Economic Development and Cultural Change* 9, 4(1961), 561–72, or Keren, M.: On the Tautness of Plans. *Review of Economic Studies* 39, 4(1972): 469–86.

7   See Ward, B.: *The Socialist Economy*. New York: Random House, or Hlaváček, J., Tříska, D.: *Úvod do mikroekonomické analýzy*. Praha: Fakulta sociálních věd UK, 1991, pp. 101–7.

8   Hlaváček, J., Zieleniec, J.: Trh práce v ekonomice, přecházející od plánu k trhu—teoretická východiska. *VP* No. 379. Praha: Ekonomický ústav ČSAV, 1991, pp. 21–23.

9   Becker, G. S.: The Theory of Social Interactions. *Journal of Political Economy* 82, 6(1974): 817–26.

10 For more details see section 10.2.1.4.

1.2 MINIMIZATION OF THE SUBJECTIVE PROBABILITY OF ECONOMIC EXTINCTION

If we admit that the economic criterion arises as a result of Darwinian natural selection, every successful economic agent (i.e. every agent that survives in the long run) tries (at least intuitively) to avoid situations involving a high risk of extinction. Therefore, we have chosen minimization of the (subjective) probability of extinction as the agent's general decision-making criterion. It can be assumed that in a liberal market environment such a criterion will be established by natural selection: agents that do not behave in this way will become extinct.

If a decision-taker feels that a low amount of funds is the sole threat to his existence, he will react to this threat with economic behaviour that can be explained using the standard neoclassical *homo economicus* paradigm, i.e. he will maximize his profit or disposable income.

If the individual feels that inferior social status is part of the threat, he will endeavour to increase his social prestige (i.e. to augment his human and social capital, in Becker's terminology). A non-profit university threatened by loss of accreditation because professors are leaving their posts will reduce this risk by increasing their pay. An individual who feels that a threat to other members of society is a threat to society as a whole and therefore also to himself will eliminate this perceived threat by behaving altruistically in society.

An economic agent usually faces not just one threat, but numerous different ones. If a producer's profit is too low, its owner may depart or it may go bankrupt. If its wages are too low, its employees may quit or the quality of its workforce may fall too low. If its price is too high, its sales may be too low. If its share of the market is too small, it may not be able to sign a sales agreement with a monopsonistic buyer. Its managers may instinctively reject a rapid change in production conditions as an inestimable risk. From the manager's point of view, operating at the upper limits of the firm's production capacity (on the production function) may be risky: if the parameters of the firm's economic situation (which the manager cannot fully control) change only slightly, he will not be able to meet the owners' expectations and he may risk losing his lucrative position in the firm and his reputation as a successful manager (for example for failing to deliver the expected profit).

The various threats perceived by a decision-taker or a group (managers, employees, owners) involved in settings the economic agent's criterion are often simultaneous and sometimes contradictory. If an agent knows how to estimate his probability of economic extinction for each individual threat, he can combine those probabilities (for example by summing them if the threats are mutually independent), thereby converting all the threats into a single scalar cardinal criterion, namely the probability of extinction of the agent due to materialization of any of the threats under consideration. Such a criterion, combining all the threats perceived by the decision-taker, then often leads to the optimal solution within the set of feasible solutions of the model. This optimal solution is often a trade-off.

Suppose that an agent's survival (or the threat to his existence) depends solely on his income, or rather on his income relative to the subsistence level: the closer the agent is to the subsistence level, the higher is his probability of (economic) extinction and so the stronger is his subjective feeling of being personally threatened.

Like profit (but unlike consumer utility), the subjective probability of personal survival is a cardinal utility function. In deterministic models we can get by with an ordinal utility function. However, in situations of a stochastic nature (such as the St. Petersburg paradox covered in Chapter 2 or the principal–agent problem discussed in Chapter 3) we cannot get by with an ordinal utility function and we can view a cardinal criterion as being an advantage in this regard.

In most chapters we will assume that the subjective probability of survival is directly proportional to the margin relative to the boundary of the extinction zone (i.e. relative to the subsistence level). This assumption is consistent with an asymmetric Pareto probability distribution.

1.3 PARETO DISTRIBUTION OF THE PROBABILITY OF SURVIVAL

The Pareto probability distribution was originally intended to represent the allocation of wealth in an economy. Later on it was used to describe, among other things, the health structure of populations of individuals, the uneven distribution of human settlement, the frequency of occurrence of individual words in a text when decoding secret messages, and the size distribution of sources or deposits of raw materials. In physics it has been used to describe certain phenomena at temperatures close to absolute zero. In all these applications it has the advantage of being asymmetric.

1.3.1 FIRST-ORDER PARETO PROBABILITY DISTRIBUTION

If we assume that an agent's probability of survival is directly proportional to the ratio of his margin (relative to the extinction zone boundary b) to his income d, we arrive at a first-order Pareto probability distribution[11] with the asymmetric distribution function:

---

11   Outside economics the first-order Pareto probability distribution is sometimes called the Bradford distribution.

$$F(d)=0 \qquad \text{for} \quad d \leq b,$$

$$F(d)=\frac{d-b}{d} \qquad \text{for} \quad d > b.$$

The probability density function for this probability distribution has the following shape:

$$f(d)=0 \qquad \text{for} \quad d < b,$$

$$f(d)=\frac{b}{d^2} \qquad \text{for} \quad d \geq b.$$

The plots of the probability distribution function $F(d)$ and the probability density function $f(d)$ for the first-order Pareto probability distribution with a unit extinction zone boundary b are shown in Figure 1.

Figure 1: The first-order Pareto probability distribution with certain-extinction-zone boundary $b = 1$

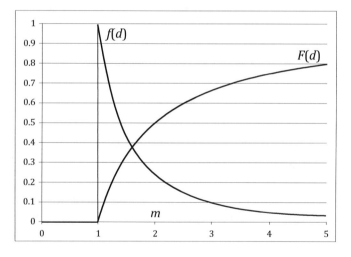

The first-order Pareto probability distribution has a zero probability for income at or below the subsistence level b and a probability converging to one as income tends to infinity. Unlike higher-order Pareto distributions, the first-order Pareto distribution does not have a final mean or variance. Its median is $m = 2b$.

We use the first-order Pareto distribution to express the subjective probability of survival in most chapters of our book. Only in the final chapter, where preferences are the deciding factor for the survival of politicians and those preferences are linked to growth in (rather than the level of) the standard of living, do we work with the assumption that the probability of survival is directly proportional to the derivative of the relative margin with respect to income. This assumption is consistent with the second-order Pareto probability distribution.

1.3.2 SECOND-ORDER PARETO PROBABILITY DISTRIBUTION

According to the psychological Weber–Fechner law[12] individuals in many cases decide not according to the intensity of a stimulus, but according to the change in the intensity of the stimulus. Individuals' assessment of their own satisfaction is often derived from the dynamics rather than the level of a utility indicator (wealth, threat): people in societies with low but rising living standards paradoxically tend to be more satisfied than those in societies with higher but flat or falling living standards. The incorporation of this law into the problem of economic threat (or the subjective feeling of threat) leads to the assumption that the subjective estimate of the probability of personal extinction is linked

not directly with the relative margin $1 - \dfrac{b}{d}$, but with its derivative $\left(1 - \dfrac{b}{d}\right)' = \dfrac{b}{d^2}$.

So, if it is true that the determining factor for the strength of the subjective feeling of threat is the increase (decrease) in the margin relative to the subsistence level in response to a (small) unit change in income, the second-order Pareto probability distribution is the right one to use for the distribution of the subjective probability of extinction. For this distribution it holds that the risk of extinction decreases in proportion to the square of the distance from the extinction zone.[13] In this case the distribution function representing the probability of survival is

$$F(d) = 0 \qquad\qquad \text{for} \quad d < b,$$

$$F(d) = 1 - \left(\frac{b}{d}\right)^2 \qquad \text{for} \quad d \geq b.$$

and the probability density function for this distribution has the following shape:

$$f(d) = 0 \qquad\qquad \text{for} \quad d < b,$$

---

12   See, for example, Frank, R. H.: *Microeconomics and Behavior*. New York: McGraw-Hill, 1994, chapter 8, p. 276.

13   Whereas for the first-order Pareto distribution the risk of extinction decreases in proportion to the distance from the extinction zone.

$$f(d) = \frac{2}{b} \cdot \left(\frac{b}{d}\right)^3 \qquad \text{for} \quad d \geq b.$$

Figure 2 shows the probability density function $f(d)$ and the distribution function $F(d)$ for the second-order Pareto distribution.

Figure 2: The probability density function $f(d)$ and distribution function $F(d)$ for a second-order Pareto distribution with extinction-zone boundary $b = 1$

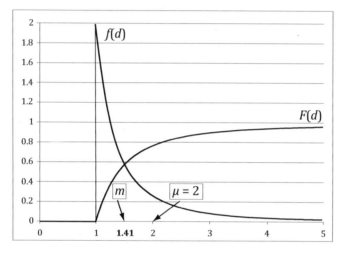

The second-order Pareto distribution has a zero probability for income not exceeding the boundary of the survival zone and a probability converging to one as income tends to infinity. It has mean $\mu = 2b$ and median $m = b \cdot \sqrt{2}$. This distribution does not have a final variance.

1.3.3 GENERAL PARETO PROBABILITY DISTRIBUTION

The general Pareto distribution of order α[14] with boundary b has the distribution function

$$F(d) = 0 \qquad \text{for} \quad d < b,$$

$$F(d) = 1 - \left(\frac{b}{d}\right)^\alpha \qquad \text{for} \quad d \geq b.$$

---

14   When used for the distribution of wealth this parameter is called the Pareto index.

The probability density function of this distribution has the shape:

$$f(d)=\frac{\alpha}{b}\cdot\left(\frac{b}{d}\right)^{\alpha+1} \qquad \text{for} \quad d \geq b,$$

$$f(d)=0 \qquad\qquad\qquad \text{for} \quad d < b.$$

The mean for second- and higher-order Pareto distributions is

$$\mu=\frac{\alpha \cdot b}{\alpha-1}.$$

The standard deviation of a Pareto distribution of order $\alpha \geq 3$ is

$$\sigma=\left(\frac{b}{\alpha-1}\right)^{2}\cdot\frac{\alpha}{\alpha-2}.$$

We obtain the Dirac delta function $\delta(d-b)$ from the α-th-order Pareto distribution function as the limiting case for $\alpha \to \infty$.

The following figure compares Pareto distributions of various orders and the Dirac delta function:

Figure 3: Comparison of the characteristics of Pareto distributions of orders 1, 2 and 3 with extinction zone boundary $b = 1$ (the dotted line shows the Dirac delta function $\delta(d-b)$)

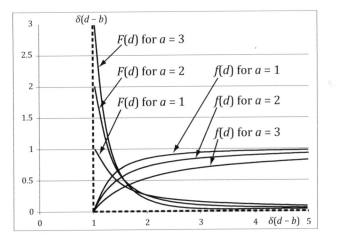

2.

MODELLING RISK
AND HEDGING AGAINST IT

Daniel Bernoulli[15] (1700–1782) is credited with creating the model of maximization of the expected payoff[16] in the modelling of economic decision-making under risk. Numerous experiments have demonstrated that this approach does not fully correspond to agents' economic behaviour.[17] The assumption that the criterion of a rational agent in a situation of uncertainty is maximization of expected profit can also be easily challenged in other ways than on the basis of empirical experience.

One of the most effective ways of challenging the expected payoff maximization model is the "St. Petersburg paradox", where the profitable strategy for each player is one which brings him success in an absolutely negligible percentage of cases and in practically no case leads to a large loss.

The hypothetical game is as follows: A player pays, say, a million dollars to enter a casino (the St. Petersburg casino) where only one game is played—a coin is tossed repeatedly until it lands heads. Let us denote this number of

---

15 Nephew of the more famous Jacob Bernoulli (1654–1705), who among other things developed the law of large numbers.

16 See Bernoulli, D.: Specimen theoriae novae de mensura sortis. Originally published in 1738; English translation: *Econometrica* 22, 1(1954): 23–36. Bernoulli himself claimed that this model was known long before his time.

17 See, for example, Mosteller, F., Nogee, P.: An Experimental Measurement of Utility. *Journal of Political Economy* 59, 5(1951): 371–404, or Kahneman, D., Tversky, A.: Rational Choice and the Framing of Decisions. *Journal of Business* 59, 4(1986): 251–78.

tosses by n. The player then receives 2^n dollars, i.e. two dollars if he is unlucky and a head appears on the first toss, four dollars if a head appears on the second toss, and so on. The expected payoff in the St. Petersburg casino tends to infinity:

$$v_n = \frac{1}{2} \cdot 2 + \frac{1}{2^2} \cdot 2^2 + \cdots + \frac{1}{2^n} \cdot 2^n = n.$$

$$\lim_{n \to \infty} v_n = \infty$$

The payoff will exceed the million dollar entry fee if the coin lands tails twenty times in a row. The entry fee should be worth paying (in terms of the expected payoff) whatever the amount (even if it is a million dollars). However, no one with any sense will pay more than a hundred (or even, in most cases, more than ten) dollars to enter this hypothetical casino. The intuitive maximum acceptable entry fee for the basic (minimum) win of two dollars ranges between four and eighty dollars.[18]

For an expected-payoff-maximizing player, the model "profitability" of the entry fee—whatever the level—results from an astronomically high payoff in a virtually negligible number of cases. No real decision-taker will be guided by the expected profit in this case: a willingness to accept an astronomically high entry fee would evidently mean loss of the instinct of self-preservation and therefore also of the agent's (economic) viability.

The view from the "opposite side" is equally convincing—it is not profitable to run the St. Petersburg casino at zero or even negative rent if the decision is based on expected profit.[19] Meanwhile, in reality (even in the world of organized crime) there is no business opportunity that comes even remotely close to such an offer (and any economically rational agent would "take it" even at zero rent).

The questions we ask in this context[20] are the following: Does a final, economically rational price of this game exist for an economic agent? And if it does, what is that price? And which model, or which cardinal utility function, should we choose for the utility of money if we want to avoid and model the paradox described above?

The St. Petersburg paradox cannot be explained satisfactorily using "mean-variance utility" models,[21] where a weighted average of the mean and variance

18 See Maňas, M.: *Teorie her a optimální rozhodování.* Praha: Státní pedagogické nakladatelství, 1969, p. 121.

19 Negative rent here means that the operator pays nothing to the owner but instead receives a daily subsidy of a million (ten million, a billion, …) dollars from the owner on top of entry fees.

20 Hlaváček, J., Hlaváček, M.: Petrohradský paradox a kardinální funkce užitku. *Politická ekonomie* 52, 1(2004): 48–60.

21 See, for example, Meyer, J.: Two-Moment Decision Models and Expected Utility Maximization. *American Economic Review* 77, 3(1987): 422–30.

is used as the cardinal utility function. Here, again, it turns out (nonsensically from the real-world perspective) that for any non-zero weight of the mean, any entry fee to the St. Petersburg casino—whatever the amount—is acceptable.

One possible approach to explaining the St. Petersburg paradox is von Neumann's theory of expected payoff utility maximization.[22] This model uses the cardinal money utility function, which for a risk-averse agent is strictly concave. It can take the form of, for example, a power function

$$u(x) = x^\alpha \qquad \text{for} \quad 0 < \alpha < 1.$$

The field of psychology offers a different approach, namely the aforementioned Weber–Fechner law, according to which a real agent decides not according to the intensity of a stimulus, but according to the change in its intensity. The corresponding utility function is logarithmic:

$$u(x) = \alpha \cdot \log x,$$

For this function, the expected utility is proportional to α:

$$\sum_{i=1}^{\infty} \alpha \cdot 2^{-i} \cdot \log\left(2^i\right) = \alpha \cdot \log 2.$$

In both these cases (power utility function and logarithmic utility function) an appropriately sized parameter[23] (i.e. one offering a "sensible" entry fee to the St. Petersburg casino) exists. However, we have no direct economic guide (no economically justifiable direct argument) for determining this parameter, and its "appropriate" *ad hoc* setting for the St. Petersburg paradox would not be the right one for other decision-making situations.

The approaches described above share the problem that the decision does not depend on the agent's income. Yet wealth, or income, clearly does affect agents' choices in risky situations—a wealthy player will have a "lighter hand", whereas a drowning man will clutch at straws (i.e. possible but unlikely payoffs).

An alternative approach to the expected payoff utility model is to use subjective probabilities differing from the objective values. It turns out that the

---

22 See Neumann, J. von, Morgenstern, O.: *Theory of Games and Economic Behavior*. Princeton: Princeton University Press: 1953.

23 In the case of the power utility function $u(x) = x^\alpha$ the maximum acceptable entry fee lies in the "sensible" range of \$4 to \$80 for $\alpha \in \langle 0.68; 0.98 \rangle$, regardless of initial income. A similar parameter can be "set" for the logarithmic utility function.

people usually overestimate the probability of rare events.[24] This increases the value of a lottery above its expected value, every week causing millions of would-be millionaires to pay one dollar for lottery tickets having an expected payoff of 50 cents. To explain the St. Petersburg paradox, however, we would need exactly the opposite tendency, i.e. players would have to underweight (or ignore) extremely unlikely (albeit astronomically high) payoffs. This is how "real" visitors to the St. Petersburg casino think when comparing the extremely high entry fee with the expected payoff in (subjectively perceived) actually expectable cases. In so doing, they in fact "lop off" a portion of the expected payoff. We illustrate this division of the expected payoff into two parts in section 2.2 by formulating a hypothetical Leningrad casino in which the actually likely payoffs are removed and only the extremely unlikely payoffs remain. Even in the Leningrad casino, an expected-profit-maximizing agent is willing pay the entry fee whatever the amount.

We try here to build on the von Neumann–Morgenstern approach and find an economically justifiable, strictly concave cardinal utility function based on the idea of maximizing the probability of economic survival.

2.1 PROBABILITY OF SURVIVAL FOR INCOME AS A RANDOM VARIABLE

If income is a random variable we have two probability distributions to deal with—the income probability distribution and the agent survival probability distribution. By maximizing the probability of survival we arrive at a criterion reflecting the agent's risk aversion.

From the survival probability perspective, income (a random variable d having mean $\bar{d}$ and variance σ^2) that has a higher mean and a higher variance can be less advantageous than income that has a lower mean and a lower variance.

Let us assume, for example, a subsistence level of $b = 100$ money units, and let us compare income $d = 500$ with a "lottery" in which there is a 0.5 probability of winning 2000 money units (and a 0.5 probability of winning nothing). Even though the expected value of the lottery $E(d)$ is double, a survival-probability-maximizing agent will opt for certainty, because if he exchanges his entire income to take part in the lottery the expected value of his probability of survival $p(d)$ will decrease:

a) $d = 500$: $p(d) = \dfrac{d-b}{d} = \dfrac{500-100}{500} = 0.8$,

---

24   See Preston, M. G., Baratta, P.: An Experimental Study of the Auction-Value of an Uncertain Outcome. *American Journal of Psychology* 61, 2(1948): 183–93.

b) $d \in \{0; 2000\}$ with 50% probability for both alternatives:

$$p(d) = \frac{1}{2} \cdot \frac{2000 - 100}{2000} = 0.475 < 0.8 .$$

The survival-probability-maximizing agent is therefore risk-averse. We will explore how much he is willing to pay to enter the St. Petersburg casino. First, though, we will analyse his willingness to enter a less attractive casino which, however, also has an infinite expected payoff.

2.2 FORMULATION OF THE LENINGRAD CASINO PROBLEM

We start by modifying the rules slightly. In our "Leningrad casino" a player gets nothing if the coin does not land heads at least 31 times in a row. Otherwise the rules are the same as in the St. Petersburg casino. Even this disadvantageous game has an infinite expected payoff of $2^{-31} \cdot (1 + 1 + \cdots + 1 + \cdots)$, so for an expected-income-maximizing agent it should be attractive whatever the entry fee is.

Let us denote the payoff by v and the Leningrad casino entry fee by y. Let us first assume that $y \le d - b$, i.e. the player may only gamble the excess of his income over the subsistence level.

If the player loses, paying the Leningrad casino entry fee will have reduced his probability of survival by

$$\frac{d-b}{d} - \frac{d-b-y}{d-y} .$$

A rational decision-taker will compare this fall in the agent's probability of survival in the no-win scenario with the probability of winning, which would mean guaranteed survival (as a consequence of the astronomically high payoff). We ask: What is the maximum casino entry fee Y which the agent is willing to pay? For a survival-probability-maximizing agent the following must hold:

$$2^{-30} \ge \frac{d-b}{d} - \frac{d-b-Y}{d-Y} .$$

Let us denote the ratio of income to the subsistence level by $k = \frac{d}{b}$. Therefore,

k is a measure of the agent's economic situation. After a simple rearrangement we obtain:

$$Y \le \frac{b \cdot k^2}{k + 2^{31}} .$$

We will begin by estimating the fee that is acceptable to agents with income lying between the subsistence level and double that level, i.e. $1 < k < 2$. For these poor people (let's say that $k = 2$ is the poverty line) the maximum acceptable fee is less than $4b \cdot 2^{-31}$, i.e. a tiny fraction of the subsistence level (for example, less than 1 cent given a subsistence level of $10,000). Normal poor people, therefore, will not be frequent the Leningrad casino.

What is the approximate fee for an extremely rich person (let's say someone with an income that is 100 times the subsistence level, i.e. $k = 100$)? Even for him the figure is not astronomically high—the maximum acceptable fee is less than one one-hundred-thousandth of the subsistence level (10 cents given a subsistence level of $10,000). Even the rich will not visit the Leningrad casino in this model.

Nevertheless, we can theoretically consider agents who will find the Leningrad casino attractive. If we drop the assumption of $y \leq d - b$, we can take into account a desperate man whose only hope is to win, as his income is below the subsistence level: $d \leq b$, i.e. $k \leq 1$. For this agent, risky action is his only chance of survival. Moreover, this is in fact a case of moral hazard, because he is gambling with someone else's money (for example, a governmental or municipal support fund for the down and out). Even a low probability of survival is better than a zero probability, so he is willing to pay his entire income d (if he doesn't play, he won't survive anyway). The relation between the maximum acceptable entry fee and the agent's income is shown in Figure 4.

Figure 4: The maximum acceptable Leningrad casino entry fee Y versus the agent's income d (b is the subsistence level)

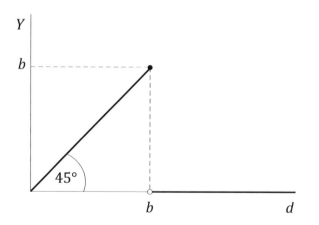

So, only down-and-out individuals with income $d \in (y, b)$ will enter the model Leningrad casino. If the entry fee is increased above the subsistence level, i.e. if $y > b$, no one will enter at all.[25]

So, if we disregard the possibility of entry by down-and-outs with a negligible probability of economic survival, we can say that the Leningrad casino is not attractive at any price.

2.3 MODEL OF THE ST. PETERSBURG PARADOX

We now return to the original problem. Players who would be influenced by the high payoff in the event of 31 or more tails would also visit the Leningrad casino. In the previous section we practically ruled out the possibility of rational agents visiting the Leningrad casino. We are therefore left only with those attracted by "normal" payoffs in other (less unrealistic) cases. The expected value of such a payoff is

$$v_{30} = \frac{1}{2} \cdot 2 + \frac{1}{2^2} \cdot 2^2 + \cdots + \frac{1}{2^{30}} \cdot 2^{30} = 30.$$

The subjective probability of survival of an agent with income equal to k-times the subsistence level b after paying Y to enter the St. Petersburg casino is not influenced by the highly unlikely, astronomically high payoffs for 31 or more tails, since the 30th tail—with a win of 2^{30}—has already guaranteed his survival with a probability of at least 99.999%.

If the coin came down heads every time in the first i tosses, the agent has income equal to $d - Y + 2^i = k \cdot b - Y + 2^i$. His probability of survival in this case is

$$\frac{d - b - Y + 2^i}{d - Y + 2^i} = 1 - \frac{b}{k \cdot b - Y + 2^i}.$$

The player's expected probability of survival if the coin comes down heads no more than thirty times in a row is therefore:

$$\sum^{30} 2 \cdot \left[1 - \frac{}{k \cdot b - Y +} \right].$$

The maximum acceptable fee is the one for which this expression equals

$$\frac{d - b}{d} = \frac{k - 1}{k} = 1 - \frac{1}{k},$$

---

i.e. the probability of survival if the agent does not enter the casino:

$$\frac{1}{k}-1+\sum_{i=1}^{30}2^{-i}\cdot\left[1-\frac{b}{k\cdot b-Y+2^i}\right]=0. \qquad (*)$$

Let us denote the left-hand side of this equation as:

$$f^{k,b}(Y)=\frac{1}{k}-1+\sum_{i=1}^{30}2^{-i}\cdot\left[1-\frac{b}{k\cdot b-Y+2^i}\right].$$

As can be seen from the following Figure 5 and Figure 6, equation (*) has a single solution in the "sensible" (i.e. economically interpretable) part of the domain:

Figure 5: Plots of $f^{k;100}(Y)$ for $k \in \{1.1; 2; 5\}$. For $k \geq 10$ the graph is virtually coincident with the x-axis on the scale used

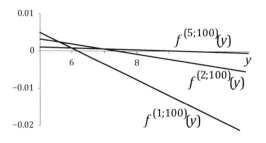

Figure 6: Plots of $f^{2;b}(Y)$ for $b \in \{100; 200; 500\}$

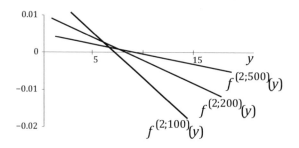

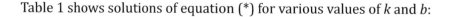

Table 1 shows solutions of equation (*) for various values of k and b:

Table 1: Maximum acceptable St. Petersburg casino entry fee Y versus agent's economic situation (i.e. versus k) and versus extinction zone boundary b

k	$b = 100$	$b = 200$	$b = 500$
1.1	6.6	7.45	8.7
2	7.35	8.25	9.5
3	7.9	8.8	10.1
4	8.25	9.2	10.5
5	8.55	9.5	10.8
10	9.5	10.5	11.8
20	10.5	11.45	12.8
30	11.05	12.05	13.35
40	11.45	12.45	13.75
50	11.8	12.8	14.1
60	12.05	13.05	14.35
75	12.35	13.35	14.65
100	12.8	13.75	14.95

Source: Authors' calculations

Figure 7 presents the maximum acceptable fee Y as a function of the agent's economic situation (parameter k, representing the ratio of income to the subsistence level) for three different extinction zone boundaries: $b \in \{100; 200; 500\}$.

Figure 7: The maximum acceptable St. Petersburg casino nominal entry fee Y versus the agent's economic situation k (b is the extinction zone boundary)

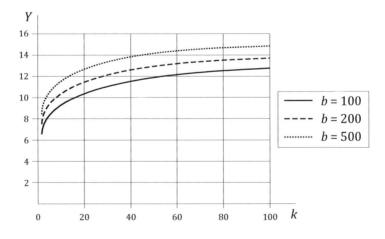

In all cases the function is growing and concave. The agent reacts positively (with higher demand) to improvements in his economic situation, but the rate of growth of the maximum acceptable fee slows with increasing k.

The relation between the maximum acceptable fee and the magnitude of b is also expressed by a growing concave function. This relation may seem surprising at first glance: growth in b means *ceteris paribus* a deterioration in the agent's economic situation, since it increases his probability of economic extinction. However, it is important to realize that the level of the threat is given by the magnitude of the relative margin $k = \dfrac{d}{b}$ and that moving to higher b while keeping k constant means not only an increase in the subsistence level, but also, (i) an equal percentage rise in income, and (ii) an "inflationary" fall in the real value of both the payoff and the entry fee. If $b = 100$ and $d = 2b = 200$, a basic (i.e. minimum) payoff of 2 represents 1% of income and an entry fee of 10 is 5% of the agent's income, whereas if $b = 500$ and $d = 2b = 1000$, the basic payoff is 0.2% of income and the same nominal entry fee 10 is 1% of the agent's income. A greater percentage of income means a greater threat, so this "inflation" leads logically to the agent accepting a higher nominal, but lower real, entry fee when faced with an greater threat (due to growth in b). This relation is shown in Figure 8, where $Y(b)$ is the maximum acceptable nominal entry fee and $(Y/d)(b)$ is the maximum acceptable real fee, in both cases as a function of the subsistence level b for an agent whose income is equal to double the subsistence level ($k = 2$).

Figure 8: The relation between St. Petersburg casino entry demand and the extinction zone boundary level for an agent with economic situation $k = 2$

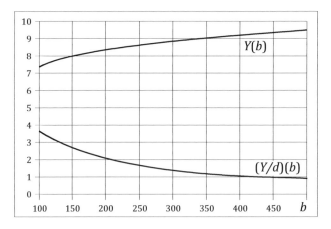

Table 2 shows how our extinction-threat-minimizing agent reacts if the game is "cut short" by the setting of a maximum number of tosses (we denote this number by N). The calculation results show that agents with the lowest income ($k \leq 1.1$) take no account of extreme profit opportunities with a probability of 2^{-12}, i.e. 0.02 %, whereas agents with extremely high income ($k \geq 50$) react more sensitively to phenomena with a probability of 2^{-20}, i.e. 0.0001%. This is in line with reality—poor people tend to play cheap games with relatively low payoffs, whereas wealthy people are attracted to games with high entry fees and high payoffs and are deterred by games with upper limits (see the lower right-hand area of Table 2, where the equation does not have an economically interpretable solution).

Table 2: Maximum acceptable entry fees for agents with various economic situations for a maximum of N consecutive favourable outcomes ($b = 100$)

k	$N = 30$	$N = 25$	$N = 20$	$N = 15$	$N = 12$	$N = 10$
1.1	6.60	6.60	6.60	6.60	6.55	6.45
2	7.35	7.35	7.35	7.35	7.25	6.95
5	8.55	8.55	8.55	8.50	7.95	6.20
10	9.50	9.50	9.50	9.20	7.10	–
50	11.80	11.80	11.55	–	–	–
100	12.80	12.80	11.80	–	–	–

Source: Authors' calculations

A survival-probability-maximizing agent therefore realistically accepts an entry fee to the St. Petersburg casino (with no limit on the number of tosses) of between \$6.60 and \$12.80 depending on his economic situation. It turns out to be irrelevant whether the agent takes into consideration the possibility of winning only when the coin lands heads 25 times or less, or even when the number of consecutive tails is greater than 25, not only because astronomically high payoffs have an extremely low probability, but also because for a lucky agent who wins \$$2^{25}$ any subsequent win will not affect his (almost unity) probability of survival. For poor agents the same holds for payoffs associated with an initial series of 15 or more successful tosses of the coin.

A normal agent with an income of double the subsistence level is willing to pay around 3.7% of his income for a chance at winning. By contrast, an agent in an excellent economic situation of ten times the subsistence level is willing to pay only around 1.0% of his income.

Things are different for down-and-out agents, whose probability of survival is zero if they do not enter the casino, i.e. for agents with an income-to-subsistence-level ratio of $k \leq 1$. As in the Leningrad casino, the optimal strategy of these agents is unique. Even for agents who can only afford the entry fee and nothing else (i.e. $d - Y = 0$), entry to the casino offers a non-zero probability of economic survival (for $b = 100$ the probability is 2^{-7}, i.e. just under one per cent). Such agents have a situational attraction (negative aversion) to risk—their situation forces them to take risks (even if they are risk averse in normal situations).[26]

And how does interest in entering the casino change *ceteris paribus* with nominal payoff amount? Suppose that the payoff is $v \cdot 2^i$, where i is the number of successful tosses (the coin lands heads i times in a row), hence $2v$ is the lowest payout (when the coin lands heads on the first toss and tails on the second). We solve the equation:

$$\frac{1}{k} - 1 + \sum_{i=1}^{30} 2^{-i} \cdot \left(1 - \frac{b}{k \cdot b - Y + v \cdot 2^i}\right) = 0.$$

We again summarize the solution of this equation for various values of v (the basic payoff amount) in a table:

Table 3: Effect of multiplying payoffs on the maximum acceptable entry fee (for $k = 2$ or $k = 5$ and $b = 100$)

v	$k = 2$	$k = 5$
1	7.35	8.55
1.1	7.97	9.31
1.2	8.56	10.01
1.5	10.27	12.07
2	12.97	15.33
3	17.98	21.40
5	26.98	32.44
7	35.16	42.54
10	46.43	56.54
15	63.54	77.89
20	79.25	97.55
30	108.15	133.70

Source: Authors' calculations

---

26 Such agents are like the penniless man in the anecdote who, after enjoying a lavish feast in a fancy restaurant, asks whether he might pay in pearls. The head waiter says yes, so the man tells him, "Okay, bring me two more oysters and keep your fingers crossed". In other game situations, situational risk attraction can of course arise in less absurd cases. See Hlaváček, J. et al.: *Mikroekonomie soundáležitosti se společenstvím*. Praha: Karolinum, 1999, 106–8.

In the following chart we show that both cases involve a growing and concave relation:

Figure 9: The relation between the maximum acceptable entry fee and the payoff

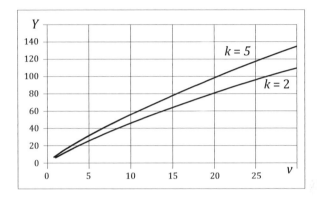

The operator of the St. Petersburg casino can therefore stimulate the interest of a survival-probability-maximizing agent by increasing the payoffs, but the marginal effect of such increases declines—increasing the payoffs thirty-fold will increase the acceptable entry fee only around fifteen-fold.

3.

MORAL HAZARD AND ADVERSE SELECTION IN THE CONTEXT OF MAXIMIZATION OF THE PROBABILITY OF ECONOMIC SURVIVAL[27]

Generally, the principal–agent problem can be described as delegated decision-making—a situation in which one economic entity (the principal) enters into an agreement (the contract) with another entity (the agent) in expectation that the agent will make decisions in the interests of the principal.

Ever since it was first formulated[28] this microeconomic theory has been developing apace.[29] However, the principal–agent principle is widely applied in other economic and non-economic areas as well.[30]

27 Hlaváček, J., Hlaváček, M.: "Principal-Agent" Problem in the Context of the Economic Survival. *Acta Economica Pragensia* 14, 3(2006): 18–33.

28 Ross, A.: The Economic Theory of Agency: The Principal's Problems. *American Economic Review* 63, 2(1973): 134–39, or Jensen, M. C., Meckling, W. H.: Theory of the Firm: Managerial Behavior, Agency Costs and Ownership Structure. *Journal of Financial Economics* 3, 4(1976): 305–60, or Frait, J.: Morální hazard a výstup z bankovního sektoru. *Finance a úvěr* 52, 3(2002): 102–4.

29 For example, Bolton, P., Dewatripont, M.: *Contact Theory*. Cambridge, MA: MIT Press, 2005, or Gintis, H: *Game Theory Evolving: A Problem-Centered Introduction to Modeling Strategic Interaction*. Princeton: Princeton University Press, 2000, or Vives, X., ed.: *Corporate Governance: Theoretical and Empirical Perspectives*. Cambridge: Cambridge University Press, 2000, or Denis, D. K., McConnell, J. J.: International Corporate Governance. *Journal of Financial and Quantitative Analysis* 38, 1(2003): 1–36, or Janda, K.: Credit Guarantees in a Credit Market with Adverse Selection. *Prague Economic Papers* 12, 4(2003): 331–49.

30 For example in macroeconomics and economic policy (Epstein, G. A., Gintis, H. M., eds.: *Macroeconomic Policy after the Conservative Era. Studies in Investment, Saving and Finance*. Cambridge: Cambridge University Press, 1995), in institutional economics (Furubotn, E. G., Richter, R.: *Institutions and Economic Theory. The Contribution of the New Institutional Economics*. Ann Arbor: University of Michigan Press,

Our approach stays strictly on the microeconomic level in its narrower sense. We discuss only those common activities of the principal and the agent which are not unrepeated trade. We also restrict our analysis to the case of just one principal. That way we avoid the problem of conflicting interests of different principals—if the agent has more than one principal, each with different interests and a different relation towards risk, then even if he wants to act in the best interests of all of those principals, this is not possible to achieve.

The principal–agent microeconomic problem could refer, for example, to the relation between:

- owner and manager,
- employer and employee,
- creditor and debtor,
- firms where one firm delegates work to another (as a subcontractor or as part of a collaborative effort),
- landowner and tenant,
- litigant and counsellor,
- investor and portfolio manager,
- managing centre and subsidiary division within one company or in a centrally planned economy,
- banking supervisor and regulated bank,
- risk-averse insuree and risk-neutral insurer,
- customer (for example of a retail chain) and supplier.

3.1 PRINCIPAL–AGENT MODEL

The decision-making interaction between the principal and the agent can be described and modelled in the following way. Let us suppose that the agent is deciding about a decision variable e and that this decision determines the outcome $x = x(e, \theta)$, where θ is a random variable with a known probability distribution.

If the principal is fully informed about the possible alternative decisions and their implications, he can force the agent to make the decision that is op-

---

1997, or Spulber, D. F.: *Market Microstructure: Intermediaries and the Theory of the Firm.* Cambridge: Cambridge University Press, 1999), in corporate governance theory (Mejstřík, M.: Corporate Governance, Ownership Concentration and FDI in CR. In *Corporate Restructuring and Governance in Transition Countries*, edited by B. Dallago and I. Iwasaki, 65–90. London: Palgrave, 2007), in the political sciences (Laffont, J. J.: *Incentives and Political Economy.* Oxford: Oxford University Press, 2000, or Arrow, K. J. et al., eds.: *Barriers to Conflict Resolution.* New York: Norton, 1995), in sociology (Cook, K. S., ed.: *Trust in Society.* New York: Russell Sage Foundation, 2001) or in the theory of law (Adler, M. D., Posner, E. A., eds.: *Cost-Benefit Analysis: Legal, Economic, and Philosophical Perspectives.* Chicago: University of Chicago Press, 2001, or Polinsky, A. M., Shavell, S.: The Economic Theory of Public Enforcement of Law. *Journal of Economic Literature* 38, 1(2000): 45–76).

timal from the principal's point of view. In the case of decision-making under uncertainty (as is usual in the real economy), the agent usually has information superiority (so-called hidden information), for example about the available technology. A common feature of principal–agent situations is the endeavour of the principal to prevent the agent from abusing this information superiority to the principal's detriment.

The principal knows that this hidden information θ is known to the agent, but he cannot get it from him. The agent makes his decision with knowledge of the value of θ, while the principal can observe neither e nor θ. The principal can therefore try to convince the agent to reveal true value of θ.

3.1.1 ADVERSE SELECTION

If, for example, an insured party—unlike the insurance company—knows his risks, this can lead to "adverse selection"[31]: commercial insurance tends to be used above all by customers who are unprofitable from the point of view of the insurance company. This is because customers—unlike the insurance company—have information about their accident probability. The uninformed insurance company has to choose the halfway (averaged) price, which is attractive for the riskiest customers but deters the least risky ones. The insured are therefore more risky than the average population. This applies not only to the insurance market—many new customers of dating agencies have found that the supply of potential partners offered by these agencies is *ceteris paribus* worse than that in the average population. Generally, adverse selection can be described as a situation in which "undesirable" customers (from the point of view of the principal) are more likely to participate in voluntary exchange.

For simplicity we assume the same initial income of $y_i = y$ for all n agents (insured parties) ($i = 1,..., n$). All agents are considered to be risk neutral with an identical utility function $v_i(y) = y$. Moreover, those agents face an identical loss $L_i = L$. The size of the loss L here (unlike in the moral hazard model discussed in the next section) is an exogenous variable which the agent cannot influence. We also assume that among the customers there are:

- $(1 - \gamma) \cdot n$ high-risk individuals who have a high accident probability π_h,
- $\gamma \cdot n$ low-risk individuals with a low accident probability π_l, where $\pi_l < \pi_h$.

---

31   This term was first used in Rothschild, M., Stiglitz, J. E.: Equilibrium in Competitive Insurance Markets: An Essay on the Economics of Imperfect Information. *Quarterly Journal of Economics* 90, 4(1976): 629–49.

Suppose that the principal (insurance company) is risk neutral and that he knows the shape of the agent's utility function $v(y) = y$ and his initial income y, the size of the potential loss L, the proportion of low-risk customers $\gamma \in (0; 1)$ and the accident probabilities of both types of customers π_h and π_l, but he is not able *ex ante* to recognize the type of customer. This prevents the principal from charging high-risk types a premium of $p_h = \pi_h \cdot L$ and low-risk types a premium of $p_l = \pi_l \cdot L$; such insurance would correspond to the expected loss and, under perfect information, would be Pareto optimal[32] for all parties.

Moreover, if the insurance company offered the "halfway" insurance premium given by the weighted average of the optimal premium for high-risk and low-risk individuals (with the weights given by the ratio of high-risk to low-risk agents), i.e. a premium of

$$p = \gamma \cdot p_l + (1 - \gamma) \cdot p_h,$$

it could be sure that only the high-risk agents would accept the offer (i.e. adverse selection would occur) and that it would make a loss. This is true for every "pooling" (same for all agents) contract. There cannot be a competitive equilibrium with a pooling contract—in the competitive equilibrium the insurance company neither generates a loss nor loses customers to its competitors, so the expected profit for a randomly chosen customer has to be equal to zero. Competitive equilibrium therefore has to generate zero profit, which cannot be true for any pooling contract.

In this case the insurance company has to offer two different ("separating") insurance contracts in such a way that would "unmask" the agent's choice of contract. These insurance contracts will differ not only in premium amount, but also in the level of coinsurance. A high-risk customer will incline towards the contract with lower coinsurance and thus with higher insurance cover.

Let us characterize these two insurance contracts by binary vectors (p_l, q_l) (the contract designed for low-risk customers) and (p_h, q_h) (the contract designed for high-risk customers). The first component of the vector describing the insurance contract represents the premium amount and the second component represents the amount the insured party will receive in the event of an accident. We will denote the utility of the agent connected with contract (p, q) by $V(p, q)$.

For the insurance company it is necessary that its customers choose the contracts that are designed for them. To ensure this the following "self-selection" constraints have to be fulfilled:

---

32   Just to clarify, it is important to distinguish rigorously between Pareto optimality and the Pareto probability distribution. These are completely different categories. Pareto optimality is the situation where no agent can become better off without making another agent worse off. The Pareto distribution is an asymmetric probability distribution and is described in Chapter 1.

$[V_h(p_h, q_h) \geq V_h(p_l, q_l)]$ & $[V_l(p_l, q_l) \geq V_l(p_h, q_h)]$.

The second of these constraints can be omitted as inactive. It would be profit-able from the insurance company's point of view for low-risk agents to choose the "stricter" contract, but rational agents will choose the more favourable con-tract (p_l, q_l). The insurance company therefore has to secure itself only against high-risk customers, so only the first constraint is active:

$V_h(p_h, q_h) \geq V_h(p_l, q_l)$.

This constraint should ensure that high-risk agents do not accept the contract which gives an advantage to low-risk agents. The self-selection constraint here—given the agents' assumed risk neutrality, i.e. $v(y) = y$—is therefore:

$$(1 - \pi_h) \cdot (y - p_h) + \pi_h \cdot (y - L + q_h - p_h) \geq (1 - \pi_h) \cdot (y - p_l) + \pi_h \cdot (y - L + q_l - p_l).$$

On the other hand, competition leads to the insurance company offering the best (from the point of view of the high-risk agent) contract with zero expected profit; otherwise a rival insurance company would take away its customers.

The expected utility of a principal that does not know the risk profile of its customer is:

$$\gamma \cdot [(1 - \pi_l) \cdot (y - p_l) + \pi_l \cdot (y - L + q_l - p_l)] + (1 - \gamma) \cdot [(1 - \pi_h) \cdot (y - p_h) + $$
$$+ \pi_h \cdot (y - L + q_h - p_h)].$$

By maximizing this function subject to the self-selection constraint it can be proved[33] that for the principal the best separating contract for high-risk cus-tomers is

$(p_h, q_h) = (\pi_h \cdot q_h, L)$,

which is the same as the contract under perfect information—full cover at a price equal to the expected loss. The optimal separating contract for low-risk agents has to have only partial cover $(q_1 < L)$ and its premium is equal to the expected value of the insurance contract:

$p_l = \pi_l \cdot q_l$.

However the existence of such a competitive equilibrium is not assured. It de-pends on the proportion of low-risk customers γ. If it is higher than some trig-

---

33   See Gravelle, H., Rees, R.: *Microeconomics*. London: Longman, 1992.

ger value γ^*, there will be a pooling equilibrium (where the insurance company offers one contract to all) with zero expected profit and this equilibrium will drive separating contracts from the market. Nevertheless, as discussed above, no pooling contract can be an equilibrium. Thus, no competitive equilibrium exists in this case.

If $\gamma \in (0; \gamma^*)$ the existence of a competitive equilibrium is assured with suitable separating contracts. However, even here this equilibrium is not Pareto optimal. Compared with the case of perfect information, insurance companies are equally well off (zero profit), high-risk agents are not better off either, but low-risk agents are in a worse situation, so the equilibrium cannot be Pareto optimal. Therefore, either a competitive equilibrium does not exist at all, or it is not Pareto optimal.

3.1.2 MORAL HAZARD

In the other basic principal–agent model—the "moral hazard" model[34]—the agent takes his decision e before he knows the value of the random variable θ, and the principal can observe neither the agent's decision e, nor the value of the random variable θ, but only the outcome of the agent's activity x. In this case the principal cannot force the agent to choose the decision e which would be the best from the principal's point of view. Consequently, the principal will enforce a contract rewarding the agent according to the outcome x. This results in a situation (as in the adverse selection model) where a competitive equilibrium either does not exist or is Pareto inefficient.

Let us describe this model in greater detail for the case of one agent (and one principal, i.e. as assumed throughout this chapter).

Let us assume again that the principal is risk neutral and competitive (i.e. he is satisfied with zero expected profit as he does not want to lose a customer). Contrary to the model in the previous section the expected loss is endogenous to the model (i.e. it is affected by the decision of the agent).

We assume that the agent (let's say an insured party) can—but does not have to—spend c money units to reduce the risk of loss. We also assume that the agent (unlike the principal) has information that:

- if he spends nothing (i.e. if $c = 0$), the probability of loss is $\pi_0 \in (0, 1)$,
- if he spends $c = c_1$, the probability of loss is $\pi_1 \in (0, \pi_0)$.

As in the previous section we will denote the insurance premium by p, the level of cover provided by the insurance company by q (where, of course, $q < L$) and

---

34   See Mirrlees, J. A.: *The Theory of Moral Hazard and Unobservable Behaviour. Part I.* Mimeo. Oxford: Nuffield College, Oxford University, 1975, or Holmstrom, B.: Moral Hazard and Observability. *Bell Journal of Economics* 10, 1(1979): 74–91.

the initial level of income by y. The expected income of a prudent agent who has bought cover and spent c_1 to reduce the risk is:

$$(1 - \pi_1) \cdot (y - c_1 - p) + \pi_1 \cdot (y - c_1 - p - L + q).$$

If insurance companies have the same information as the insured (i.e. if they can check whether the customer has really spent money to reduce the risk of loss), a competitive market will lead to the Pareto optimal contract with full cover ($q = L$) and with a premium of $p_0 = L \cdot \pi_0$ for imprudent customers and $p_1 = L \cdot \pi_1$ for prudent customers. The expected profit of the insurance company will be zero.

If the insurance company is uninformed and credulous, it will offer the contract ($L \cdot \pi_1$, L). For the customer it is optimal to accept this contract and to spend no money on reducing the risk, i.e. $c = 0$. The expected profit of the insurance company is negative in this case—the insurance company creates losses due to its naivety.

As uninformed but suspicious insurance company will proceed similarly as in the adverse selection model—it will offer an insurance contract with partial coverage. Less risk-averse customers will not spend money to reduce the risk and will accept a contract with full cover and a higher premium, whereas customers with high risk aversion will pay such costs and will accept a contract with partial cover. The expected profit of the insurance company is zero (as in the case of fully informed insurance companies).

By contrast, the insured is worse off than in the case of fully informed insurance companies—he has either lower cover with the same expected income, or lower expected income with full cover. As in the adverse selection model, therefore, this equilibrium is not Pareto optimal.

This model represents a kind of market failure. The state can try to rectify this failure by means of tax policy. For example, in the health insurance area it can impose higher taxes on cigarettes to stimulate spending on reducing the risk (spending on nicotine addiction therapy), or in the property insurance area it can reduce indirect taxes on alarms or locks. This can lead to an improvement in Pareto efficiency. The problem, however, is that the government needs a lot of information about the preferences and the sets of feasible solutions for the decision-making problems of economic agents in order to set the optimal tax policy. But if the principal does not have this information, the state will not have it either.

A common problem of the moral hazard and adverse selection models, then, is that it is impossible to achieve an Pareto-efficient equilibrium and even impossible to achieve a contract that is beneficial for both sides. Hence, even if a market equilibrium exists, it is not Pareto optimal.

The assumed decision-making criterion of economic agents—namely maximization of the utility of expected income—is of course crucial to these con-

clusions. We will show that the generalization of agents' decision-making criterion to maximization of the probability of survival, together with the survival of
the agent (conditional on the survival of the principal), can under some conditions guarantee the existence of a market equilibrium even in cases where such
equilibrium does not exist if we use the criterion of maximization of the utility
of expected income.

We will go on to show that the generalization of the profit-maximization
criterion to maximization of the probability of survival for agents enables us
to usefully model some situations characterized by two criteria per decision-
making problem and imperfect information of one of the economic agents, with
the interests of the principal and the agent being at least partially jointly satisfied.

3.2 APPLICATION OF GENERALIZED MICROECONOMICS: MAXIMIZATION OF THE PROBABILITY OF ECONOMIC SURVIVAL

3.2.1 THREAT TO THE AGENT DUE TO EXTINCTION OF THE PRINCIPAL

If the economic survival of the agent depends on the survival of the principal
then there is an overlap of interests of the principal and the agent—an overly
"defrauded" principal could suffer economically and even go bust. The agent
thus follows (but does not maximize) the interests of the principal in his own
interest.

In this section we assume that survival of the principal is a necessary condition for survival of the agent. This does not hold the opposite way round—the
principal survives even if the agent does not.

We assume that the agent maximizes his probability of economic survival,
while the principal endeavours to achieve at least zero expected income connected with the contract. This is a condition for competitive equilibrium, which
would occur in the case of perfect information.

As in the previous sections, however, we assume information asymmetry.[35]
The agent knows his accident probability, but the principal does not.

---

35   Daňhel, J.: K problému asymetrie informací v pojišťovnictví. *Politická ekonomie* 50, 6(2002): 809–13.

3.2.2 ADVERSE SELECTION IN THE CONTEXT OF PROBABILITY OF SURVIVAL

The principal supplies the agents with accident insurance in return for payment (the price of the contract p). We differentiate between two types of agents: high-risk and low-risk.

Similarly as in the previous section:

y_p denotes the principal's initial level of income,
y_a denotes the agent's initial level of income,
L denotes the size of the potential loss,
$\gamma \in (0; 1)$ denotes the proportion of low-risk agents with low accident probability π_l,
π_h denotes the accident probability for high-risk agents, where $\pi_l < \pi_h$,
b_a denotes the agent's extinction zone boundary,
b_p denotes the principal's extinction zone boundary.

Let us assume again that the principal is not able recognize *ex ante* the type of agent he is dealing with; he only knows the proportion of high-risk agents $\gamma \in (0; 1)$. If the principal offers a pooling contract with price p and with full cover, his expected income from the contract is:

$$y_p = \gamma \cdot (y_p - \pi_1 \cdot L + p) + (1 - \gamma) \cdot (y_p - \pi_h \cdot L + p).$$

The principal's probability of survival is

$$v_p(p) = \gamma \cdot \frac{y_p - b_p - \pi_1 \cdot L + p}{b_p} + (1 - \gamma) \cdot \frac{y_p - b_p - \pi_h \cdot L + p}{b_p}.$$

We assume that the agent cannot survive alone—if the principal perishes, the agent perishes as well:

$$v_a(p) = v_p(p) \cdot \frac{y_a - p - b_a}{b_a}. \tag{*}$$

An agent maximizing the probability of parallel survival of both entities prefers neither an extreme decrease nor an extreme increase in the price of the contract, because:

$$\lim_{p \to \infty} v_a(p) = 0,$$

$$\lim_{p \to 0} v_a(p) = 0.$$

An increase in the price of the contract p increases the first and decreases the second multiplicand in (*). The agent therefore prefers price p^* for which:

$$\frac{v_p(p^*)}{v_p'(p^*)} + p^* = b_p \cdot v_p(p^*) + p^* = y_a - b_a .$$

The important point here is that both the high-risk and the low-risk agents evaluate the situation in the same way. Both are fully insured against accidents, so they have the same second multiplicand in (*). Any accident will decrease their probability of economic survival only as a consequence of a decrease in

the probability of survival of the principal. This probability will decrease by $\dfrac{L}{b_p}$

percentage points from $\dfrac{y_p - b_p + p}{b_p}$ to $\dfrac{y_p - b_p - L + p}{b_p}$. The low-risk agents do

not leave system any more than the high-risk agents.

This means that if the survival of the agent is contingent on the survival of the principal, then the problem of adverse selection does not exist for entities maximizing their probability of economic survival.

There is even in some sense an opposite tendency. In the text below we will show that entities with well-below-average income do not demand insurance services when payment of the insurance premium increases their probability of economic extinction even if no accident occurs. An increase in the premium thus leads to an increase in the "reliability" of the insured over the average of the population (and does not decrease it below the average as in the standard adverse selection model). This is true despite the fact that the insurance is not advantageous even for the extremely well off, because they are very insensitive to changes in the premium.

An increase in the premium increases the expected income of the principal. The principal will therefore be better off if the price of the contract increases. By contrast, the number of surviving agents and demand in the insurance market are decreasing in the range $(0; p^*)$, whereas they are "modestly" increasing or constant in the range $(p^*; +\infty)$. This means that an equilibrium does not necessarily exist. This is so when $S(p^*) < D$. If an equilibrium premium does exist, then it is unique. At this price the expected profit of the principal is equal to zero.

The principal will offer full cover at a price that is higher for the low-risk agent than it would be in the case of perfect information. That notwithstanding, the agent accepts this price—from the point of view of his economic survival even the low-risk agent will be better off under these conditions.

Consequently, a competitive Pareto equilibrium may exist—neither the principal, nor the low-risk agents—and still less the high-risk agents—are worse off relative to the perfect information case.

In future research[36] we will relax the strong very assumption (*), for example in the sense that extinction of the principal only cancels the accident cover. Such a change will of course generate significant changes in the conclusions of the analysis. Nevertheless, we do not expect this to rule out the possibility of the existence of a Pareto equilibrium.

3.2.3 MORAL HAZARD IN THE CONTEXT OF PROBABILITY OF SURVIVAL

In the moral hazard model we again assume only two entities—a principal and a single agent. We consider the accident probability π to be an endogenous variable here. The agent can (but need not) spend money to reduce this probability. He will do so if it will increase his probability of economic survival. Let us denote the cost of reducing the risk by c. When the agent spends $c > 0$, the original (unreduced) accident probability $\pi(0) = \pi_0$ decreases to $\pi(c) \in (0, \pi_0)$.

We again assume that the agent cannot exist independently—if the principal perishes, the agent perishes as well:

$$v_a(c) = \left[\left((1 - \pi(c)) \cdot \frac{y_a - p - b_a}{b_a} + \pi(c) \cdot \frac{y_a - p - L - b_a}{b_a} \right) \right] \cdot v_p(c). \qquad (**)$$

The principal maximizes his expected income:

$$y_p(c) = y_p - \pi(c) \cdot L + p.$$

The probability of economic survival of the principal is:

$$v_p(c) = \frac{y_p - b_p - \pi(c) \cdot L + p}{b_p}.$$

Expenditure on reducing the accident probability will increase the principal's probability of survival:

$$c > 0 \Rightarrow v_p(c) > v_p(0) = \frac{y_p - b_p - \pi(0) \cdot L + p}{b_p}.$$

---

36 Another possible avenue of research would be to set up a model that describes the situation where the agent is simultaneously a secondary principal (for example an owner). In this scenario it is no longer clear who is the principal and who is the agent. This was the case during the Czech privatization process in the 1990s, when companies owned each other either directly or via claims exceeding the equity of the debtor. See Turnovec, F.: Who Are the Principals and Who Are the Agents? A Leontief-type Model of Ownership Structures. *Finance a úvěr* 50, 11(2000): 648–50. The standard principal–agent models (adverse selection and moral hazard) are unable to deal with this situation because they consider entities with conflicting interests.

For the agent, expenditure on reducing the accident probability reduces the first multiplicand in (**). The second multiplicand increases, so the effect of spending c on the agent's utility (i.e. on his probability of survival) is given by the difference:

$$v_a(c) - v_a(0) = \left((1 - \pi(c)) \cdot \frac{y_a - p - b_a}{b_a} + \pi(c) \cdot \frac{y_a - p - L - b_a}{b_a} \right) \cdot v_p(c) -$$

$$- \left((1 - \pi(0)) \cdot \frac{y_a - p - b_a}{b_a} + \pi(0) \cdot \frac{y_a - p - L - b_a}{b_a} \right) \cdot v_p(0) =$$

$$= \frac{y_a - p - b_a}{b_a} \cdot \left((1 - \pi(c)) \cdot v_p(c) - (1 - \pi(0)) \cdot v_p(0) \right) +$$

$$+ \frac{y_a - p - L - b_a}{b_a} \cdot \left(\pi(c) \cdot v_p(c) - \pi(0) \cdot v_p(0) \right).$$

The sign of the difference $v_a(c) - v_a(0)$ is driven by the relation of the extent of the threat to the agent and the principal. If the agent regards the principal as "indestructible", he will not spend the cost and will transfer his risk fully onto the shoulders of the principal. The agent will thus pay $v_a(c) - v_a(0) < 0$. The more endangered the principal is in the eyes of the agent, the bigger is the difference $v_a(c) - v_a(0)$. For an extremely threatened principal it certainly holds that $v_a(c) - v_a(0) > 0$. Hence, there is definitely some threshold above which the agent will not voluntarily practice moral hazard and will spend to reduce the accident probability in the interests of both parties.

3.2.4 COMPARISON OF THE STANDARD HOMO ECONOMICUS WITH A SURVIVAL-PROBABILITY-MAXIMIZING AGENT

The above analysis has demonstrated that the problem of information asymmetry (specifically, the problems of adverse selection and moral hazard) is much weaker in a model economy where agents maximize their probability of economic survival than in the standard economic climate of agents maximizing their expected profit, where the utility of the agent is in an antagonistic relationship with that of the principal.

We have shown that the adverse selection problem—where contracts are signed by the most risky agents—disappears if the survival of the agent is contingent on the survival of the principal. In fact, the opposite applies—the most risky agents do not enter into the contract because paying the premium increases their probability of economic extinction even if no accident occurs.

Under these conditions (in contrast to the standard adverse selection model) a competitive-equilibrium and Pareto-efficient pooling contract can exist where the insurance company offers one contract to all. If the survival of the agent is only partially contingent on the survival of the principal, the adverse selection problem reappears, albeit to a lesser extent than in the case of maximization of expected income.

The moral hazard problem—where the principal is unable to verify whether the agent has spent money to reduce his accident probability—also disappears to some extent. If the threat to the principal relative to the threat to the agent (in the assessment of the agent) is above a certain threshold, the agent will voluntarily spend to reduce his accident probability and will therefore not practice moral hazard.

For both models analysed (adverse selection and moral hazard) the assumed maximization of the probability of economic survival by agents implies that a Pareto-optimal equilibrium can exist with a pooling contract with full accident cover provided by the principal. This is the main difference from the standard model with decision-takers maximizing their expected income.

4.

THE DEMAND FUNCTION IN THE INSURANCE MARKET: COMPARISON OF MAXIMIZATION OF THE PARETO PROBABILITY OF SURVIVAL WITH THE VON NEUMANN–MORGENSTERN EU THEORY AND KAHNEMAN–TVERSKY PROSPECT THEORY

4.1 INSURANCE IN THE MODEL OF MAXIMIZATION OF AN AGENT'S PARETO PROBABILITY OF (ECONOMIC) SURVIVAL

To address the problem of rationality of the insured, we need to quantify the economic gain/loss associated with an agent's decision whether or not to buy insurance. We regard our generalized microeconomic theory—where the agent maximizes his probability of (economic survival)—as a suitable methodological approach in principle for examining the issue of insurance.

This utility function (in contrast to the EU theory and prospect theory—see below) reflects the fact that the agent's economic situation is the key factor for his insurance decision (and consequently for the insurance demand function). Agents with very high income will reject insurance (as an unfair game). However, agents with extremely low income will not buy insurance either, because if they did they would have to forgo other consumer goods which, from their perspective (and given their economic situation), they regard as more necessary.

As a consequence of their economic situation, agents may therefore adopt the risky strategy of "not insuring", since they "simultaneously" consider two risks: the risk of losing the item to which the insurance relates, and the risk of having insufficient "residual" income after paying the premium. Even if they are not risk-attracted, their situation can force them to take risks.[37]

Throughout this chapter we assume that the agent must cover any loss immediately. This means that an insurance loss represents not only a loss of wealth, but also a loss of income. This simplifying (but acceptable at the level of abstraction of this book) assumption will allow us to avoid complications linked with the relationship between the wealth and income of the agent.

Let us assume that the agent is considering insuring against a loss of L money units and that the probability of loss is p and the insurance premium is a. The expected loss is $E(L)$ money units. For insurance companies to be able to exist, the premium must be higher than the expected loss: $a > E(L)$. The agent's income is d. We will denote his subsistence level (the boundary of his economic extinction zone) by b. We assume that the agent will not cross this boundary if he pays the premium: $a < b - d$.

We assume that demand for insurance is driven by the number of agents whose risk of economic extinction will be reduced by buying insurance. If an agent does not take out insurance, he will save a money units for the premium but he will face the risk of losing L money units with a loss probability of p.

The key factors in this decision include not only the premium amount a, the loss probability p and the related loss L, but also the agent's income d, or rather his income relative to the boundary of the economic extinction zone b. These are the variables that determine his survival probability. We assume that the agent is price taker as regards the premium offered. He therefore has just two options:

A. To insure by paying the premium of a money units. His risk of (economic) extinction (resulting from a decline in his income below the subsistence level b) is then:

$$R_1(d) = \frac{b}{d-a}.$$

B. Not to insure. In this case his risk of extinction (due to loss L with probability p) is:

$$R_2(d) = p \cdot \frac{b}{d-L} + (1-p) \cdot \frac{b}{d}.$$

The key factor in the agent's insurance decision is the difference $R_1(d) - R_2(d)$. If it is positive the agent will not take out insurance because the risk of economic extinction associated with paying the premium exceeds the risk of loss. Such

---

37 See footnote 26 in section 2.3 for more on the issue of agents being forced into taking risks by their situation.

a loss might be highly unpleasant (or even ruinous for very poor people), but is relatively highly unlikely.

The illustrative plots in Figures 10, 11, and 12 provide a comparison of the model agent's strategy to insure with his strategy not to insure (for three different premiums). The agent's income is represented on the horizontal axis. If, for income d, the plot of function $R_1(d) - R_2(d)$ lies above the horizontal axis, i.e. if $R_1(d) > R_2(d)$, it is profitable for the agent to take out insurance at a premium of a.

Figure 10: Graph of function $R_1(d) - R_2(d)$: comparison of the probability of extinction (in %) with insurance at a premium of $a = 60$ money units and with no insurance ($b = L = 250$)

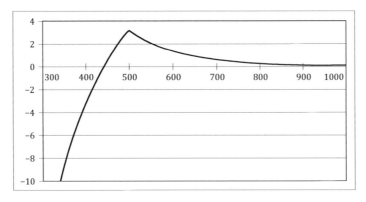

Figure 11: Ditto for a premium of $a = 70$ money units

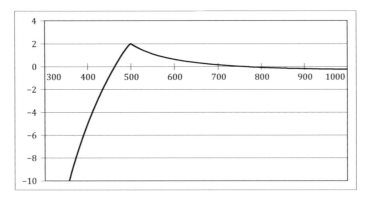

Figure 12: Ditto for a premium of $a = 80$ money units

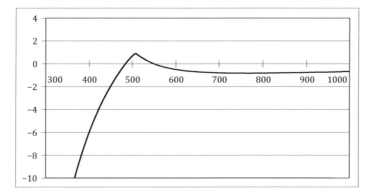

To be able to derive the shape of the insurance demand function $D(a)$, all we need to do now is introduce an assumption about the income distribution in the relevant population. For now we will limit ourselves to the simplest uniform income distribution over the range (b, δ), where δ is the highest income in the system. If the entire plot of the function $R_1(d) - R_2(d)$ lies below the horizontal axis over the entire domain (b, δ), it is not profitable for any agent to take out insurance, i.e. $D(a) = 0$. If this is not the case, we will denote the minimum and maximum income of the insured with premium a by $d_1(a)$ and $d_2(a)$ respectively. The value of the demand function $D(a)$ will then correspond to the ratio of the length of the range $(d_1(a), d_2(a))$ to the spread of the incomes in the system:

$$D(a) = \frac{d_2(a) - d_1(a)}{\delta - b}.$$

In the illustrative cases depicted in the following two graphs (Figures 13 and 14) we assume $\delta = 4b$, i.e. a uniform income distribution over the range $(b, 4b)$. The corresponding insurance demand function is plotted in Figure 13:

$$D_1(a) = \frac{d_2(a) - d_1(a)}{3b} \qquad \text{for } a \le 80,$$

$$D_1(a) = 0 \qquad \text{for } a > 80.$$

Figure 13: The insurance demand function in the survival probability maximization model with uniform income distribution over the range (b, $4b$)

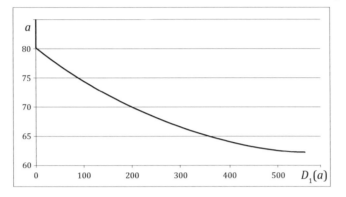

Figure 14 shows the agents for which taking out insurance is the less risky strategy (in the sense of the probability of economic extinction) in the given situation at various premiums. If point (d, a) lies in the grey region Q, an agent with income d regards premium a as an acceptable offer. It can be seen from Figure 14 that agents with very low income ($d < 300$) will not accept even a fair game, i.e. one where the premium equals the expected insurance claim $a = 50$, whereas the rather better off will even accept a premium that is higher than the expected claim. Agents with extremely high income, however, will reject the game even when the premium slightly exceeds the expected loss. In the real insurance market, though, the premium always exceeds this level, as otherwise insurance companies would be loss-making.

Figure 14: Income characteristics of insurance demand in the survival probability maximization model: agents for whom (a,d) $\in Q$ will take out insurance

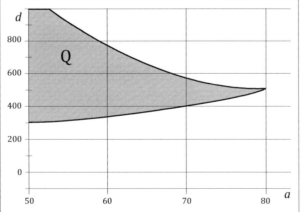

In the following two sections (4.2 and 4.3) we will construct the insurance demand function for the two most common approaches to modelling an agent's relationship to risk. We will work first of all with von Neumann and Morgenstern's assumption of expected utility maximization (EU theory) and then with Kahneman and Tversky's prospect theory. At the end of Chapter 4 we will compare the insurance demand function $D_1(a)$ constructed under the assumption of economic survival probability maximization with the demand functions constructed using EU theory and prospect theory.

4.2 INSURANCE DEMAND IN THE VON NEUMANN–MORGENSTERN MODEL OF MAXIMIZATION OF THE EXPECTED UTILITY OF INCOME (EU THEORY)

In the von Neumann–Morgenstern model[38] a rational economic decision is one which maximizes the expected utility of the economic gain, not the expected gain itself (i.e. the gain multiplied by the probability of success). An economically rational agent experiences a diminishing marginal utility of money (income), i.e. for $j > k$ the number of utils (i.e. subjective utility units) he derives from the j-th money unit is smaller than the number of utils he derives from the k-th money unit.

As in the previous section, the agent decides whether it is profitable for him to take out insurance at a premium of a money units against a loss of L money units that will occur with a probability of p. The expected loss is $E(L)$ money units. We assume again that the premium a is higher than the expected loss: $a > E(L)$.

The illustrative example used for the following graphs considers a potential loss of $L = 250$ money units and a loss probability of $p = 0.2$. The expected loss due to theft is therefore $E(L) = 50$ money units and the premium a is alternatively in the range of 50–80 money units. In this illustrative example we assume an income utility function in the form $u(d) = 1000 \cdot \sqrt[4]{\dfrac{d}{1000}}$.

From the utility maximization perspective, the relationship between utility and income for insurance is determined by the money (income) utility function. As we are entering the domain of stochastic phenomena here, we naturally need to use cardinal utility in order to be able to quantitatively compare the expected utility of insurance cover with the loss associated with paying the

38   See Neumann, J. von, Morgenstern, O.: *Theory of Games and Economic Behavior*. Princeton: Princeton University Press, 1953.

premium. A key assumption of the model is that the income utility function is strictly concave, characterizing risk-averse agents. Given the description of insurance this assumption is certainly more than acceptable.[39]

Figure 15: The Von Neumann–Morgenstern model of the expected utility of money: the poorer the agent, the greater the loss of utility generated by a loss of 250 money units

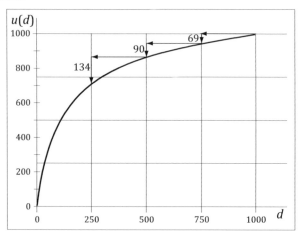

The question is whether an economically rational agent will pay the premium of a money units. If he does, he will experience a fall in income of a money units. If he does not, his expected income will decrease by $E(L)$ money units. For all agents, expected income is *ceteris paribus* higher in the no-insurance case. If decision-takers were by guided by expected income, no one would take out insurance.

How will the situation change if we work not with expected income, but with the expected utility of income? We will assume a universal (identical for all agents) income utility function $u(d)$.

We will assume $d \geq a$. Otherwise the decision-taker would not even consider insurance.

A loss of L money units will give the agent a decrease in utility of a magnitude that depends on his level of income. This can be seen on the graph—in the event of an insurance loss an agent with an income of $d = 1000$ money units loses 69 utils, whereas an agent with an income of 750 money units loses 90 utils. An agent with an income of 500 money units would lose 134 utils.

---

39   A risk-averse agent will reject all games with a zero expected payoff (fair games), but he will also reject some games with a positive expected payoff if the payoff is so low that it does not offset the decrease in utility associated with the negatively perceived risk [i.e. with the non-zero variance of random variable $u(d)$].

The loss associated with paying a premium of 60 money units is also different for agents with different income levels: $u(1000) - u(940) = 15$ utils, $u(750) - u(690) = 19$ utils, and $u(500) - u(440) = 27$ utils.

An agent with an income of $d = 1000$ money units therefore has a utility of $u(940) = 985$ utils when insured and an expected utility of $0.8 \cdot u(1000) + 0.2 \cdot u(750) = 0.8 \cdot 1000 + 0.2 \cdot 930 = 986$ utils when uninsured. He will therefore decide not to buy insurance. By contrast, an agent with a lower income of $d = 500$ money units has a utility of $u(440) = 814.4$ utils when insured and an expected utility of $0.8 \cdot u(500) + 0.2 \cdot u(250) = 0.8 \cdot 841 + 0.2 \cdot 707 = 814.2$ utils when uninsured. Consequently, it is profitable for him to be insured. The same thinking will also induce an agent with a low income of $d = 310$ money units to opt for insurance (with a greater incentive than an agent with income of $d = 500$ money units), as he has a utility of $u(250) = 707$ utils when insured and an expected utility of $0.8 \cdot u(310) + 0.2 \cdot u(60) = 696$ utils when uninsured.

In this model of maximization of the expected utility of income it is irrational for the wealthy (from a certain income level upwards) to be insured, whereas for poorer people it is irrational not to be insured.[40]

The threshold case (the threshold income level d_1) is the level at which an economically rational agent ceases to insure himself given an increment in his income. The threshold d_1 is the root of the equation[41]:

$$h(d) = p \cdot u(d-L) + (1-p) \cdot u(d) - u(d-a) = 0.$$

We can interpret function $h(d)$ as a measure of the strength of the incentive to insure. For a strictly concave and growing utility function $u(d)$, equation $h(d) = 0$ has a single solution and the income threshold d_1 is therefore unique. In our illustrative example depicted in Figure 16 the threshold is $d_1 = 522$ money units.

So, with a premium of $a = 60$ money units, agents with income $d < 522$ will take out insurance and agents with higher income will not.

For different premiums the willingness to buy insurance and the threshold income level both decrease. Figure 17 illustrates the relation between the income threshold (the income above which agents do not buy insurance) and the premium amount. Insurance is bought by agents below the income threshold $d \le d_1$, for which (d, a) lies within Q.

What is the income elasticity of demand in this expected utility maximization model? Demand is given by the premium multiplied by the number of agents below the income threshold d_1 (which is constant given constant preferences).

---

40   Only, of course, if they can afford to pay the premium of a. We assume they can.
41   In our illustrative example the equation is $0.2 \cdot u(d - 250) + 0.8 \cdot u(d) - u(d - 60) = 0$.

Figure 16: The income threshold d₁ in the model of maximization of the expected utility of income: root of equation $h(d) = 0$

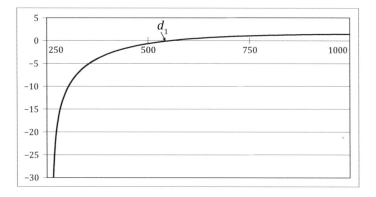

Figure 17: The relation between the income threshold d_1 in the model of maximization of the expected utility of income and premium amount *a*

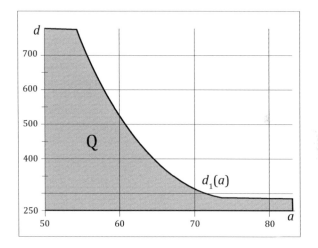

We will denote the relation between insurance demand and income by $D(d)$. An increase in income of 1% will cause a decrease in the number of agents below the income threshold, so the income elasticity is negative. Insurance is an inferior good:

$$E_D^d = d \cdot \frac{D'(d)}{D(d)} < 0.$$

Let us now explore the price elasticity of demand

$$E_D^a = a \cdot \frac{D'(a)}{D(a)} < 0$$

for our example. The graph in Figure 18 below plots the insurance demand function in the case of a uniform income distribution.[42]

Figure 18: The insurance demand function $D_2(a)$ in the von Neumann–Morgenstern model of maximization of the expected utility of income

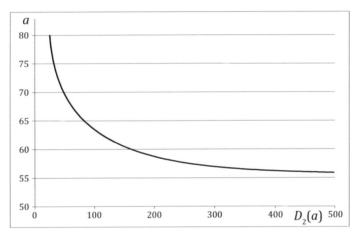

Figure 19 shows the high elasticity of this demand function over its entire domain. The elasticity at point $T \equiv [a; D(a)]$ is given by the segment ratio TL/TK, which is greater than 1 for the entire demand curve.

Figure 19: Elasticity of the insurance demand function: segment ratio TL/TK

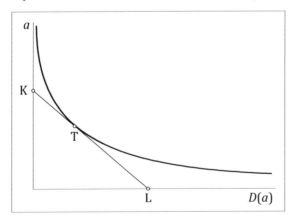

---

42 With probability density function $f(d)$ constant in the range $I \equiv (M, 4M)$ and zero for $d \notin I$.

In this expected income utility maximization model, therefore, insurance demand is price elastic for all premium levels. The elasticity decreases with premium price.

In von Neumann and Morgenstern's EU model, insurance is simultaneously an inferior good, as it is demanded by low-income agents (hence an increase in income will reduce demand), and a luxury good, as agents react very sensitively to a rise in the price.

These properties of the EU model are realistic for high and medium levels of income: the better off such an agent is, the less attractive to him is insurance at an unfair price (i.e. a price exceeding the expected loss, a condition that always applies in the insurance market, as otherwise insurance companies would loss-making).

The model is unrealistic[43] for agents with very low income d, who would be left with virtually no income after paying the premium. In reality such agents will not buy insurance, because paying the premium worsens their economic situation, thereby reducing their subjective satisfaction to a greater extent than the risk of an uninsured loss. A very poor person who inherits a property or a car will not insure it, because he would face economic collapse after paying the premium. He compares the risk of losing the item with the risks associated with experiencing a relatively significant fall in the money he needs to pay for the bare necessities, and he chooses to reject the offer of insurance.

Another problem with the expected utility of income model—as pointed out by economic psychologists[44]—is the imperfect additivity of economic preferences. Contrary to economic rationality, people code their expenditure according to purpose (food, housing, insurance) and do not always sum their gains and losses in these sub-items.[45] Moreover, people tend not to value an economic action in the same way when it is broken down into multiple actions with the same aggregate gain/loss—people are more willing to pay a high price when it is broken down into several smaller amounts than when they have to pay it all in one go.[46] Consequently, the time distribution of payments plays a role in the insurance decision—a customer of an insurance company will more hap-

---

43 See also Skořepa, M.: Zpochybnění deskriptivnosti teorie očekávaného užitku. *WP IES* No. 7. Praha: Fakulta sociálních věd UK, 2006, pp. 1–15.

44 See, for example, Tversky, A., Kahneman, D.: Judgment under Uncertainty: Heuristics and Biases. *Science* 185, 4157(1974): 1124–31, and Frank, R. H.: *Microeconomics and Behavior*. New York: McGraw-Hill, 2006, pp. 259–83.

45 Tversky, A., Kahneman, D.: The Framing of Decisions and the Psychology of Choice. *Science* 211, 4481(1981): 453–58.

46 For instance, a lunch with a split price for the main dish and side dish ($8 + $2) is psychologically more acceptable than the same lunch at an aggregate price ($10). In this context, Richard Thaler formulated two pragmatic rules for making commercial offers more attractive: segregate gains ("Don't wrap all your Christmas presents in one box") and integrate losses (a hot tub seems cheaper if it is bundled into the price of a home than when valued in isolation). See Thaler, R. H.: Mental Accounting and Consumer Choice. *Marketing Science* 4, 3(1985): 199–214.

pily accept insurance paid for on an ongoing basis than insurance paid for in a lump sum "upfront". And when paying on an ongoing basis he willingly accepts a higher price than predicted by the von Neumann–Morgenstern expected utility maximization model. Hence, the imperfect additivity of preferences in the Kahneman–Tversky model affects the subjective degree of risk aversion.

Another tricky issue is the ability of agents to assess objectively the loss probability and its potential impacts on their utility. Tversky showed that people frequently displayed intransitivity of preferences when making choices under uncertainty,[47] while Edwards found significant differences between subjective and objective probabilities.[48]

Interesting experiments have been conducted with deferred gratification, i.e. with the inclusion of the time factor in insurance decision-making. A preference for immediate consumption over deferred consumption means a decrease in the weight of future uncertainty and can lead to subjective underweighting of the level of risk. This phenomenon was studied by, among others, Friedman.[49] In his permanent income theory, consumers adjust their savings so as to keep their income constant over their lifetime. Future consumption is discounted at a subjective risk underweighting rate, which Friedman estimated at at least 30% (and substantially higher when inflation is in double figures). This causes risk to be underweighted in the insurance decision as well.

An interesting way to explain certain phenomena in the area of choice under uncertainty that are inconsistent with standard economic models (including the von Neumann–Morgenstern EU model) is asymmetric valuation of personal income. This is described in the next section.

4.3 INSURANCE DEMAND IN THE KAHNEMAN–TVERSKY MODEL (PROSPECT THEORY, PT)

Psychologists have observed that people often assess their economic situation based not on their absolute income, but rather on the change therein or on deviations from their starting position.[50] Kahneman and Tversky's prospect theory takes this aspect of the human psyche into consideration.[51] In this theory the utility function:

---

47 See Tversky, A.: Intransitivity of Preferences. *Psychological Review* 76, 1(1969): 31–48.

48 See Edwards, W.: The Theory of Decision Making. *Psychological Bulletin* 51, 4(1954): 380–417.

49 See Friedman, M.: Windfalls, the "Horizon" and Related Concepts in the Permanent Income Hypothesis. In C. F. Christ et al., *Measurement in Economics*, Stanford: Stanford University Press, 1963.

50 The aforementioned Weber–Fechner law from psychology—see section 1.3.2.

51 See Tversky, A., Kahneman, D.: The Framing of Decisions and the Psychology of Choice. *Science* 211, 4481(1981): 453–58, and Tversky, A., Kahneman, D.: Judgment under Uncertainty: Heuristics and Biases. *Science* 185, 4157(1974): 1124–31.

a) is strictly convex in the region of losses relative to a reference point (inflection point R in Figure 20 below) and strictly concave in the region of gains relative to the same reference point. This corresponds to an assumption of decreasing sensitivity to a stimulus as the stimulus gets more intense, i.e. an assumption of decreasing marginal utility from a growing gain and a decreasing marginal loss as the loss increases;[52]

b) is steeper in the loss region than in the gain region, i.e. the decrease in utility given a loss of a unit of income is greater than the increase in utility given a gain of a unit of income. This is consistent with the fact that decision-takers assign a greater weight to a loss than to an equal gain.[53]

What we have, then, is an asymmetric utility function that displays risk aversion in the region of gains and risk attraction in the region of losses relative to the reference point, which is the inflection point of the function.[54]

The Kahneman–Tversky utility function in Figure 20 is consistent with this— a nominally smaller loss has a greater effect on the agent's utility than a nominally larger gain in the agent's wealth, i.e. even though $a > |b|$, $u(a) < |u(b)|$.

Figure 20: The Kahneman–Tversky utility function

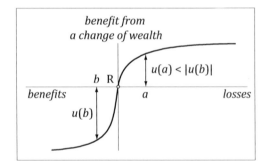

52   In the later cumulative prospect theory the assumptions of a convex-concave utility function are modified in the sense that the concavity changes into convexity and vice versa when there is a very low probability of an extreme outcome. See Skořepa, M.: Daniel Kahneman a psychologické základy ekonomie. *Politická ekonomie* 52, 2(2004): 247–55.

53   Kahneman and Tversky derived the shape of the utility function from empirical findings, according to which the steepness of the utility function in the loss region is around 2.2 times greater than in the gain region. For comparison, in section 4.4, where we compare the EU model (section 4.2), the Kahneman–Tversky prospect theory (section 4.3) and the Pareto survival probability maximization model (section 4.1), we use the same utility function in the gain region as in the previous section, i.e.

$u(d) = 1000 \cdot \sqrt[4]{\dfrac{d}{1000}}$ for $d \geq 0$, and in the loss region we assume a constant aversion to loss relative to gain: $u(d) = -2.2 \cdot u(-d)$ for $d < 0$.

54   In a later version of their theory (known as cumulative prospect theory, CPT) the authors responded to new empirical findings by making the shape of the value function dependent on the magnitude of the probability of the gain or loss and differentiating between the risk relationships for normal deviations and extreme deviations from the reference point.

The degree of convexity/concavity decreases with distance from the reference point R. This is in line with psychological findings[55] according to which the impact on the human psyche of a unit marginal increase in a stimulus declines as the strength of the stimulus increases.

Besides the utility function, a key factor in Kahneman and Tversky's theory for choice under uncertainty is the conversion of objective probabilities into subjective ones. Economic psychology has demonstrated that people tend to overweight the probability of extremely unlikely events and underweight the probability of normal phenomena. Prospect theory captures this using a weighting function that converts the objective probability of a phenomenon p into a subjective probability $\pi(p) = \dfrac{p^\delta}{\sqrt[\delta]{p^\delta + (1-p)^\delta}}$, where $\delta \in (0;1)$ is the parameter determining the degree of overweighting of the probability.[56]

For example, for an agent with property d who is able to buy insurance at a cost of a against a loss of L with a probability of p, the key relation in Kahneman and Tversky's prospect theory is[57]

$$\pi(p) \cdot u(d - L) \sim [1 - \pi(p)] \cdot u(d - a).$$

This value function in Kahneman–Tversky prospect theory is therefore a modified utility function. For "sensible" values of δ (i.e. for values consistent with the degree of overweighting of insurance loss probabilities in the hundreds of per cent at most), the function is still convex-concave and still steeper in the loss region than in the gain region.

The higher sensitivity to losses than to gains implies that a "fair" game (for instance tossing a coin, where both the magnitude and probability of gain and loss are equal) is acceptable to our model agent—he does not perceive it to be detrimental. This attitude to risk influences his insurance choice—a potential insurance loss of b money units has a larger weight in his decision than a potential increase in wealth of a money units saved on the premium and he is willing to buy insurance at a premium substantially higher than the expected loss. For such an agent, it is not profitable to choose coinsurance at a reduced premium, whereas in the case of the standard strictly concave utility function

55 See Frank, R. H.: *Microeconomics and Behavior*. New York: McGraw-Hill, 2006, chapter 8, 259–83.

56 Kahneman and Tversky again derived the shape of the weighting function $\pi(p)$ from empirical findings. For the following comparison we use a value of $\delta = 0.7$, at which the overweighting of a phenomenon with a probability of 1% is roughly fourfold ($\pi(0.7) = 3.8$). This value may be appropriate for the decision to buy insurance (where the loss probability is in whole percentage numbers), but is not so for the decision to buy a lottery ticket (where the probability is several orders of magnitude lower).

57 Likewise, for the decision to buy a lottery ticket at price q with payoff V with probability p, the key relation for the Kahneman–Tversky utility function is $\pi(p) \cdot u(d + V) \sim [1 - \pi(p)] \cdot u(d - q)$.

such coinsurance would be seen as worthwhile.[58] Using the Kahneman–Tversky value function we can also explain the economically irrational tendency to take sunk costs into account when making decisions[59]—out-of-pocket expenditure (albeit in the past) is regarded as a loss, whereas opportunity costs are seen as (less valued) foregone profits.

The Kahneman–Tversky value function is sensitive to the ranking of alternatives. Pooled profits and losses are assessed more favourably than profits and losses considered separately. Even merely changing the sequence in which problems are solved changes the assessment.

Figure 21: The Kahneman–Tversky value function for a very poor agent—such an agent will not take out insurance

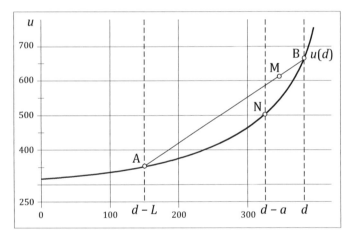

Figure 21 shows the insurance threshold for the Kahneman–Tversky value function in prospect theory. There is a fundamental difference here from the analogous function in the previous section: people above the threshold take out insurance. Poorer agents have negative risk aversion (a strictly convex utility function) and are therefore risk seekers, i.e. they do not eliminate risk with insurance. The threat (with a $1:5$ probability) of a loss of $L = 250$ money units corresponds to point M, which is one-fifth (since $p = 20\%$) of the way along AB, closer to d. This point lies above $N \equiv [d - a, u\,(d - a)]$ for every sensible premium, i.e. for every premium that is higher than the expected loss $E(L)$ and lower than the potential loss L (in our case for $50 \leq a < 250$). Any agent below the

---

58   See Frank, R. H.: *Microeconomics and Behavior*. New York: McGraw-Hill, 1994, chapter 8, 259–83.

59   Sunk costs are costs that have already been incurred and cannot be affected by the agent's current choice. He should therefore not take them into account when making his decision.

point of inflection of the Kahneman–Tversky value function in prospect theory will reject insurance because he is risk-attracted.

An agent whose income will—even after paying the premium—remain above the point of inflection of the Kahneman–Tversky value function but who would be driven below this point by an insurance loss (into the negative risk aversion region) can be described as "middle class". Such an agent is depicted in Figure 22.

Figure 22: The Kahneman–Tversky value function for a middle-class agent—such an agent will take out insurance

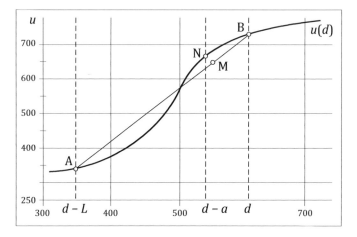

For wealthy agents the situation is the same as in the previous section: given extremely high income (above the threshold) insurance ceases to be worthwhile.

The attitude to insurance of an agent with a Kahneman–Tversky utility function therefore differs from that of an agent maximizing the expected utility of wealth primarily in the case of agents with below-average income. In the previous model the poor chose insurance, whereas as here they do not. As for wealthy agents, their strategy differs from the previous model only in that the wealth threshold above which agents take out insurance can increase. This will happen if the threshold is just above the point of inflection of the Kahneman–Tversky curve.

The insurance demand function here is significantly less price elastic compared to the expected utility of wealth maximization approach. A poor agent is a risk-seeker (has negative risk aversion) and so does not react to a reduction in the premium. The threshold above which a wealthy agent will take out insurance is determined more by the position of the reference (inflection) point than by the premium amount.

The insurance market in the Kahneman–Tversky model has lower and less price elastic demand than the previous model. Conversely, the income elasticity of demand is higher for the Kahneman–Tversky asymmetric value function, because as income increases some agents move into the category of wealthy agents, who, unlike poorer ones, are risk averse. The Kahneman–Tversky value function therefore exhibits particularly high income elasticity in the vicinity of its point of inflection.

In the expected utility of wealth maximization model we observed a paradoxical view of insurance among the poorest (the poor have more insurance the poorer they are), whereas the Kahneman–Tversky approach succeeds in capturing the aversion to insurance that exists among the poor in reality. However, the motive—negative risk aversion—is debatable. This trait may exist in the poorer classes with regard to gambling, for example, but it is more than debatable in the case of insurance. Moreover, in the Kahneman–Tversky model even the middle classes do not buy insurance, whereas in reality they account for most of the demand for insurance. Insurance is taken out by agents lying above the threshold $d \geq d_2$ and below the threshold $d \leq d_1$ for which point (a, d) lies in region Q in the following figure.

Figure 23: Wealth thresholds d_1 and d_2 in the Kahneman–Tversky value function model versus insurance premium a.

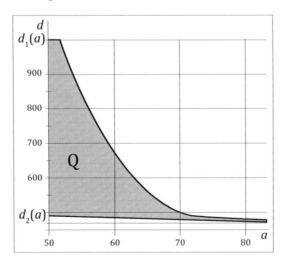

Related to this is the insurance demand function, i.e. the relation between demand and price (premium a):

Figure 24: The insurance demand function in the Kahneman–Tversky value function model with uniform income distribution

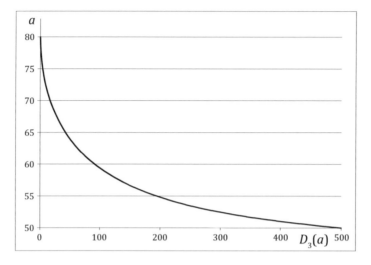

In the following section we will compare the insurance market demand curves for all three models studied (see Figures 13, 18, and 24).

4.4 COMPARISON OF THE DEMAND FUNCTIONS OF MODELS A, B, AND C (FROM THE PREVIOUS THREE SECTIONS)

The following figure compares the insurance demand functions discussed in the previous three sections.

The Kahneman–Tversky model logically displays the lowest demand at lower prices, as it excludes all agents of below-average wealth from the insurance demand (with its assumption of a positive attitude to risk in the convex left-hand part of the domain). At prices above the threshold there is zero demand.

By contrast, high prices are the least off-putting in the model of maximization of the expected utility of income, since a large proportion of agents here have a positive attitude to risk.

With an increasing premium, the survival probability maximization model will reduce insurance demand most sensitively. The expected utility maximization model of course exhibits the highest demand for agents with below-average income, since in this case even the poorest buy insurance. For those with above-average income the predicted reaction in the expected utility of income maximization model is similar as in the Kahneman–Tversky model, while there are more agents excluded than in the survival probability maximization model.

Figure 25: Comparison of insurance demand functions:
   $D_1(a)$**: Survival probability maximization model**
   $D_2(a)$**: Expected utility of income maximization model**
   $D_3(a)$**: Kahneman–Tversky value function model**

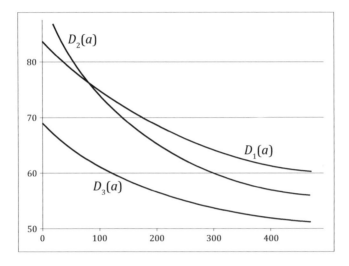

The Kahneman–Tversky model therefore shows the lowest price elasticity (over the entire domain), while insurance demand is most elastic in the von Neumann–Morgenstern model of maximization of the expected utility of income.

The following table presents a clear comparison of the analysed models with regard to the price and income elasticity of demand:

Table 4: Comparison of models according to the elasticity of demand for insurance

Model	Elasticity of insurance demand	
	Price	Income
A (von Neumann–Morgenstern)	high, insurance is a luxury good	negative, insurance is an inferior good
B (Kahneman–Tversky)	low, insurance is a difficult-to-substitute good	high, insurance is a luxury good
C (survival probability maximization)	moderate	moderate

The breakdown of insured agents by income level differs considerably across the three models under consideration. If we divide the population by income level into five classes (very poor, poor, lower-middle class, upper-middle class, very wealthy) we can say that, given a moderate ("sensible") premium a, in the model of maximization of the (declining) utility of income, insurance will be taken out by the very poor, the poor and the lower and upper-middle classes, i.e. all except the wealthiest lying above threshold $d_1(a)$ illustrated in Figure 17. In the Kahneman–Tversky value function model, insurance is purchased only by upper-middle-class agents, specifically those with income in the range of $d \in (d_{infl} + a; d_1(a))$, where d_{infl} is the point of inflection of the Kahneman–Tversky value function. If $d_{infl} + a > d_1(a)$, no one will buy insurance. In the Pareto survival probability maximization model, the poor and the lower and upper-middle classes will take out insurance.

An increasing premium will progressively deter all agents in all models, last of all the very poor in the income utility maximization model and the upper-middle class in the Kahneman–Tversky value function model. A low premium close to the expected loss $E(L)$ would be accepted by all agents in the income utility maximization model, by only the upper-middle class and the wealthy in the Kahneman–Tversky value function model, and by everyone except the extremely poor in the Pareto survival probability maximization model. This is illustrated clearly in the following table, which indicates which classes buy insurance in which models.

Table 5: Who will take out insurance in the three models under comparison?
    A – von Neumann–Morgenstern maximum utility of income model
    B – Kahneman–Tversky value function model
    C – Pareto survival probability maximization model

Classes	Premium	
	Low	**High**
very poor	A	A
poor	A, C	A
lower-middle	A, C	–
upper-middle	A, B, C	B
very wealthy	A, B, C	–

The von Neumann–Morgenstern model of maximization of the expected utility of income displays an increasing incentive to insure with falling income even for extremely badly off agents. This is unrealistic. In reality, the middle classes buy insurance. Anyone who is neither extremely wealthy nor extremely poor can (unlike the very poor) afford to pay for insurance without making any great sacrifices and is motivated to do so because (unlike the very wealthy) they would suffer a large (or even ruinous) loss in the event of accident or theft. By contrast, the very poor do not buy insurance in reality.

Both the economic survival probability maximization model and the Kahneman–Tversky model reflect the reality that the very poor are rarely insured. In the latter model, though, all economic agents with below-average income will decide against insurance (unlike in reality). The main difference between the Kahneman–Tversky model and the survival probability maximization model lies in the assumed motive for the choice "not to insure" for agents with below-average income. In the former case, the reason (plainly unrealistic in insurance-related matters) is that these agents are attracted to risk (i.e. they exhibit the negative risk aversion typical of gamblers), whereas in the latter case the reason is a lack of money, meaning either that the economic agent cannot afford the premium at all or that paying it would cause an excessive fall in his standard of living.

For the reasons given above, we regard our survival probability maximization model as being more consistent with the real-life behaviour of economic agents in the insurance market than both von Neumann and Morgenstern's income utility maximization model and Kahneman and Tversky's prospect theory.

5.
MODELLING NON-PROFIT INSTITUTIONS: THE UNIVERSITY SUPPLY FUNCTION

5.1 ECONOMIC RATIONALITY IN THE NON-PROFIT SECTOR

The problem with optimization models of non-profit organizations lies in the criterion. Profit *by definition* cannot be the criterion. The level of fulfilment of the institution's primary objective comes into consideration. For universities this means, for example, the number of students (or graduates) or the number of research outputs. There is, however, another problem (common to all optimization models)—the optimum lies on the boundary of the set of feasible solutions. This means not only the maximum possible number of students (which is itself unrealistic), but also the tightest possible budget (no reserves), the maximum possible tuition fee (not a cent less than the amount sufficient to fill the university's capacity), the minimum teachers' pay (not a cent more than the amount sufficient to retain the required number of teachers that year) and so on. Such a university would certainly lose its accreditation very quickly, because to keep that accreditation it needs some degree of tradition and stability, not-too-high turnover of teachers (especially elite ones), soundness in meeting financial obligations, and so on. A transient increase in economic indicators in the current year will endanger vitally important parameters for the next year.

That said, economic behaviour is (*again by definition*) optimizing. Economic agents behave in such a way that they choose the best solution from the feasible options. The fulfilment of this subjective optimum definitely certainly shows some common (objective) traits. The agent fulfils such criterion (even if only unconsciously or implicitly) because otherwise it would not succeed in competition with other agents.

Robert H. Frank[60] popularized Milton Friedman's idea comparing the microeconomic model of the firm to the model of play of a skilled billiards player. His play can be neatly described as the application of the law of reflection and the law of conservation of momentum. Yet the player does not mentally construct the angles or compute the momentum; he relies on intuition and experience. However, any player who plays in violation of these laws of physics will not be successful and will not be a member of the set of top players described by the model.

Another example is that of a motorcyclist leaning into a turn so that his angle respects the centrifugal force, the force of gravity and the grip of the road. In the model describing his riding style it would be necessary to sum the vectors of these forces. But the motorcyclist in the model does not sum any vectors. He rides that way because otherwise he would needlessly increase his risk of crashing.

Something similar applies to the firm: profit maximization is not always a day-to-day concern or an explicit management criterion. Nonetheless, a successful firm (one that survives economically in the face of competition) behaves in accordance with profit maximization. It arrives at such behaviour by trial and error. That is why the profit maximization model is an appropriate (and, at a certain level of abstraction, certainly the best) description of the behaviour of a firm in a competitive environment where there is a risk of extinction. We can describe the profit criterion as the "Darwinian" criterion which the firm must respect (even if not explicitly) if it is to be economically successful.

What general criterion can be used for non-profit institutions? As we explained in the introduction to this book, to model non-profit institutions (for which the profit criterion makes no sense) we can apply a more general "Darwinian" criterion—maximization of the probability of survival. This criterion must be respected by every agent operating in an economic environment where there is a risk of extinction. Again, the criterion does not have to be explicit; agents that are successful in a competitive environment implicitly respect it simply because otherwise they would not survive.

We emphasize again that this is a generalization of, not an alternative to, the *homo economicus* paradigm. The standard profit-maximizing agent is a special case of this criterion (for the profit sector in a market economy).

60   Frank, R. H.: *Microeconomics and Behavior*. New York: McGraw-Hill, 2006, p. 6.

5.2 AN OPTIMIZATION MODEL OF UNIVERSITY BEHAVIOUR

In this section we summarize the results of an analysis of the impact of various funding modalities on the behaviour of universities.[61]

We assume that every university at every stage maximizes its probability of survival. The control variables are the tuition fee and teachers' pay.

In simulation experiments using this optimization model we compare the university's behaviour and the overall market supply in the system for various different funding modalities. We will test the common assumption that the introduction of tuition fees leads to a larger supply of university places and to higher teachers' pay.

In the experiments we compare three university funding modalities which are comparable in terms of the overall amount universities receive, but different in terms of the allocation of these funds within the system. The funding modalities are the following:

- tuition fees only,
- a combination of tuition fees and subsidies,
- no tuition fees, i.e. subsidies from donors (e.g. the government) only.

In the case of subsidies we assume that the subsidy amount is directly proportional to the number of students, i.e. the donor sets a subsidy per student. Operating costs are also proportional to the number of students, while maintenance costs are proportional to the (exogenous) capacity of the university.

The management of the university seeks a strategy that (with regard to its competitors) minimizes its risk of extinction. We assume that the biggest risks of extinction faced by non-profit university organizations are:

a) excessively low teachers' pay (by comparison with the competition)— this increases the likelihood that key teachers will quit and go to work for other universities, which, in turn, may cause loss of accreditation;

b) excessively high teachers' pay—this increases expenditure, thereby increasing the likelihood that the university will go under for financial reasons;

c) a relatively high tuition fee (by comparison with the competition)[62]— this may deter students, causing the university to lose money because it is not operating at full capacity;

---

61 For detailed results of these experiments, see Hlaváček, J.: Dynamický model soustavy univerzit. *WP IES* No. 90. Praha: Fakulta sociálních věd UK, 2005, or Reichlová, N., Cahlík, T., Hlaváček, J., Švarc, P.: Multiagent Approaches in Economics. In *Mathematical Methods in Economics*, edited by L. Lukáš, 77–98. Plzeň: Západočeská univerzita, 2006, or Cahlík, T., Hlaváček, J., Marková, J.: Školné či dotace? (Simulace s modely systému vysokých škol). *Politická ekonomie* 56, 1(2008): 54–66.

62 Only, of course, if the university system is partly or fully funded from tuition fees. For the "centralist" case (subsidy funding only) risks c) and d) are not relevant.

d) a very low tuition fee—this may increase the number of applicants above the university's capacity and represents an opportunity cost (which economically rational decision-takers must always take into consideration).

In cases b), c), and d) the university's profit deteriorates, thereby increasing its probability of extinction due to financial loss or due to loss of willingness of the owner (the donor, e.g. the government) to finance an excessively (by comparison with the competition) loss-making operation.

By maximizing its probability of survival the university avoids risks a), b), c), and d) to the optimal extent. At the same time it must keep an eye on the competition. For example, if teachers' pay increases in the system, it must respond by raising pay or else it will face an increased risk of extinction due to loss of accreditation. Likewise, an increase in the average tuition fee in the system will give every university scope to increase its tuition fee the following year.

The university's optimization task each year must therefore respect:

a) the tuition fees of its competitors last[63] year,
b) the teachers' pay of its competitors last year,
c) its own (mainly capacity) constraints,
d) any changes to the subsidy regulations.

The university therefore formulates its decision-making problem only in response to past outcomes and to the decisions of its competitors and (where relevant) the donor.

The appropriate instrument for modelling the decision-making process described above would seem to be a simple system of optimization submodels for each university, with the outcomes of optimization of one sub-model influencing the other submodels in the next iteration step. We assume that average variables are taken into consideration, i.e. the university makes decisions when its tuition fee or teachers' pay is above or below the average in the system.

In its present form, the model assumes that the donor's decision regarding the parameters of the subsidy regulations is exogenous. In the model simulation experiments, any reflection of this decision must therefore be limited to analysing the sensitivity of the model (i.e. to observing the impact of changes in selected exogenous parameters on the optimum or equilibrium in the system).

We assume that every university knows:

---

63 It would be better (from the point of view of the highest possible probability of survival) for the university to know not only the past, but also the future strategy of its competitors. We do not assume this; as in the standard theory of the firm we assume that information of this type is confidential and unavailable to competitors.

- the average tuition fee in the system in the past period,
- the average teachers' pay in the system in the past period,
- the number of teachers at all universities in the system in the past period,
- the number of students at all universities in the system in the past period,
- the total student demand in the given year for the system as a whole,
- the marginal teachers' pay—when pay is at this or a lower level, the university's probability of extinction as a result of teachers quitting is 100 per cent,
- the donor's (government's) subsidy per student,
- the university's fixed costs (proportional to its capacity),
- other costs per student.

We assume two threats to the university:
- the threat of insolvency, where expenditures exceed revenues (or revenues plus reserve fund),
- the threat of loss of accreditation as a result of (elite, accreditation-enabling) teachers quitting.

The university cannot choose unilateral extremes. So, for example, while extremely low salaries (by comparison with the competition) will reduce the need for funds (and thereby reduce the threat of insolvency), they will lead to teachers quitting and thereby greatly increase the risk of extinction as a result of loss of accreditation. If the university gets part of its revenues from tuition fees, it again holds that the extreme strategy is not profitable—a sharp increase in the tuition fee may more than proportionally reduce the number of people applying to study at the university and thereby reduce its revenues. Even offering the incentive of a low tuition fee with the aim of making up revenue by attracting a large number of students will not necessarily benefit the university, as it is possible that the increase in student numbers will not cover the loss of tuition fee revenue.

As in other chapters we will assume that the probability of survival is proportional to the margin relative to the boundary of the extinction zone and can therefore be quantified using the Pareto probability distribution. In this chapter we will stay with the first-order Pareto probability distribution (see Chapter 1).

The university sets its control variables in such a way as to minimize its probability of extinction due to a decrease in a key variable below its boundary of certain extinction. The key variables are:
- the university's revenue R for the threat of insolvency,
- the number of teachers b for the threat of loss of accreditation.

The boundaries of certain extinction are:
- $R = C + F$ (where C denotes costs and F the reserve fund) for the threat of insolvency,
- $b = b_{min}$ for the threat of loss of accreditation.

The control variables are:
- the tuition fee q,
- teachers' pay m.

The time-variant variables (updated in each iteration step) are:
- the number of students at the individual universities s_i,
- the number of teachers at the individual universities b_i,
- the average tuition fee in the university education market Q,
- the average teachers' pay in the system M.

The time-invariant parameters (identical in all iteration steps) are:
- the capacity (maximum possible number of students) of the i-th university k_i,
- the total number of teachers B,
- the total study demand (total for all universities) D,
- the prescribed building and equipment maintenance costs δ relative to one (not necessarily filled) study place at the university,
- the donor's (government's) subsidy per student ε.

The university chooses its control variables (tuition fee and teachers' pay) in such a way that its decision gives it the maximum probability of survival (of all the feasible alternatives).

We assume that the feasible alternative levels of the tuition fee and teachers' pay do not differ by more than 10% from the average for the whole system in the past period. The university is in a situation of uncertainty and is "feeling its way", so its (theoretically rational) strategy is incorporated into its choice to that extent only. The university therefore regards a greater-than-10% deviation of the tuition fee or teachers' pay from the system-wide average as a *sui generis* risk. This condition will limit the possibility of having a "wall-to-wall" strategy, which is unfavourable as regards the speed of achieving equilibrium in the system.

The sets of feasible values for teachers' pay Φ_m and for the tuition fee Φ_q (identically for all universities) are therefore the 21-member sets

$$\Phi_m \equiv [0.9 \cdot M(t-1); 0.91 \cdot M(t-1); ...; M(t-1); ...;$$

$$1.09 \cdot M(t-1); 1.1 \cdot M(t-1)],$$

$$\Phi_q \equiv [0.9 \cdot Q(t-1); 0.91 \cdot Q(t-1);...; Q(t-1);...;$$

$$1.09 \cdot Q(t-1); 1.1 \cdot Q(t-1)].$$

The iterative process continues until the average tuition fee and average teachers' pay in the system repeats itself or differs by less than a specified (low) value ε (say the resolving power for teachers/study applicants) from one step to the next. Thereafter, no university has any incentive to change its choice from the previous step and equilibrium has been reached in the system.

The flow chart for this algorithm is shown on the following two pages.

We will now summarize the main conclusions from the computational experiments. Table 6 gives an overview of the main outputs (at system equilibrium, i.e. in the final iterative step, which is practically no different from the penultimate step). The final column in Table 6 shows the difference compared to the mixed variant combining government funding and tuition fees.

Table 6: Summary of results of computational experiments for comparison of alternative university funding modalities

	Funding variant	University number:				Total	Versus mixed
		1	2	3	4		
No. of students	Mixed	597	737	733	743	2 810	–
	Fees only	599	780	778	781	2 938	+128
	State only	556	754	1100	1200	3 610	+800
No. of teachers – university demand	Mixed	68	85	99	108	360	–
	Fees only	66	80	90	99	335	–25
	State only	56	76	110	125	367	+7
Tuition fee	Mixed	2.8	2.8	2.8	2.8	2.8	–
	Fees only	7.3	7.3	7.3	7.3	7.3	+4.5
	State only	0	0	0	0	0	–
Teachers' pay	Mixed	10.8	10.8	10.8	10.8	10.8	–
	Fees only	10.4	10.4	10.4	10.4	10.4	–0.4
	State only	10.5	10.5	10.5	10.5	10.5	–0.3

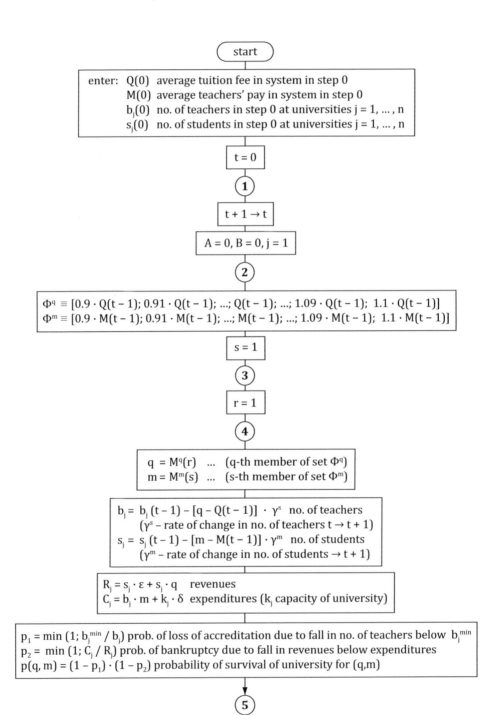

start

enter: Q(0) average tuition fee in system in step 0
M(0) average teachers' pay in system in step 0
$b_j(0)$ no. of teachers in step 0 at universities $j = 1, ... , n$
$s_j(0)$ no. of students in step 0 at universities $j = 1, ... , n$

$t = 0$

1

$t + 1 \rightarrow t$

$A = 0, B = 0, j = 1$

2

$\Phi^q \equiv [0.9 \cdot Q(t-1); 0.91 \cdot Q(t-1); ...; Q(t-1); ...; 1.09 \cdot Q(t-1); 1.1 \cdot Q(t-1)]$
$\Phi^m \equiv [0.9 \cdot M(t-1); 0.91 \cdot M(t-1); ...; M(t-1); ...; 1.09 \cdot M(t-1); 1.1 \cdot M(t-1)]$

$s = 1$

3

$r = 1$

4

$q = M^q(r)$ ... (q-th member of set Φ^q)
$m = M^m(s)$ ... (s-th member of set Φ^m)

$b_j = b_j(t-1) - [q - Q(t-1)] \cdot \gamma^s$ no. of teachers
(γ^s – rate of change in no. of teachers $t \rightarrow t + 1$)
$s_j = s_j(t-1) - [m - M(t-1)] \cdot \gamma^m$ no. of students
(γ^m – rate of change in no. of students $\rightarrow t + 1$)

$R_j = s_j \cdot \varepsilon + s_j \cdot q$ revenues
$C_j = b_j \cdot m + k_j \cdot \delta$ expenditures (k_j capacity of university)

$p_1 = \min(1; b_j^{min} / b_j)$ prob. of loss of accreditation due to fall in no. of teachers below b_j^{min}
$p_2 = \min(1; C_j / R_j)$ prob. of bankruptcy due to fall in revenues below expenditures
$p(q, m) = (1 - p_1) \cdot (1 - p_2)$ probability of survival of university for (q,m)

5

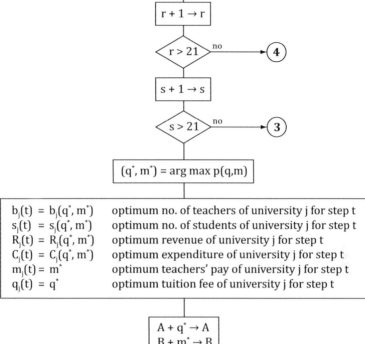

$$r + 1 \rightarrow r$$

$r > 21$ — no → ④

$$s + 1 \rightarrow s$$

$s > 21$ — no → ③

$$(q^*, m^*) = \arg \max p(q,m)$$

$b_j(t) = b_j(q^*, m^*)$	optimum no. of teachers of university j for step t
$s_j(t) = s_j(q^*, m^*)$	optimum no. of students of university j for step t
$R_j(t) = R_j(q^*, m^*)$	optimum revenue of university j for step t
$C_j(t) = C_j(q^*, m^*)$	optimum expenditure of university j for step t
$m_j(t) = m^*$	optimum teachers' pay of university j for step t
$q_j(t) = q^*$	optimum tuition fee of university j for step t

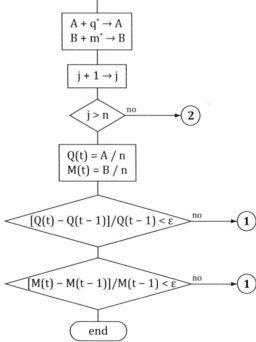

$$A + q^* \rightarrow A$$
$$B + m^* \rightarrow B$$

$$j + 1 \rightarrow j$$

$j > n$ — no → ②

$$Q(t) = A / n$$
$$M(t) = B / n$$

$[Q(t) - Q(t - 1)]/Q(t - 1) < \varepsilon$ — no → ①

$[M(t) - M(t - 1)]/M(t - 1) < \varepsilon$ — no → ①

end

82

Figures 26, 27, and 28 show the evolution of the number of students and the demand for teachers for each variant.

Figure 26: The path for tuition fee funding only (horizontal axis: iterative step number)

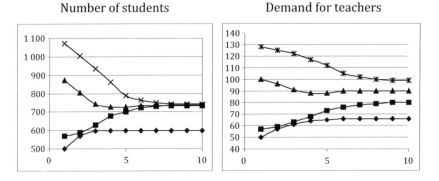

Figure 27: The path for combined funding (horizontal axis: iterative step number)

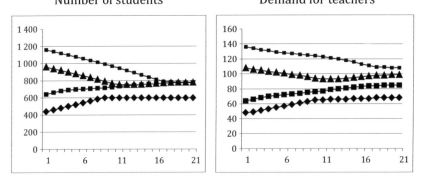

Figure 28: The path for government funding only (horizontal axis: iterative step number)

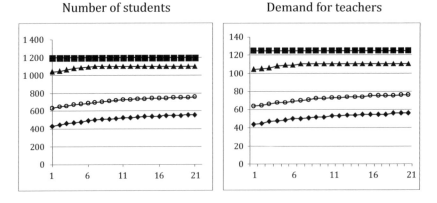

The experiments revealed that the number of iterative steps needed to stabilize the system is lowest for the liberal "tuition fee only" variant. This, however, is surprising only at first glance—both instruments for "fine-tuning" the choices of the individual universities (tuition fees and teachers' pay) are available to the full extent, whereas for the "government subsidy only" variant one of these instruments disappears, and in the mixed "tuition fee plus government sub-sidy" variant these instruments affect only part of the revenue.

Another piece of information to emerge from computational experiments not presented here is that the results are independent of the width of sets Φ_m, Φ_q, determining the permitted "force" of the iterative step. This is because the optimum was always substantially closer to the past average values for the whole system than to 10% of those average values (as used in the presented calculations).

The results of the model comparisons for the resulting variables for the system as a whole are worthy of note.

As regards the number of study applicants satisfied, the least advantageous variant is the one combining tuition fees and government funding. The high-est number of applicants is satisfied (at roughly the same costs) by the purely state-funded system. This is because of the risk of extinction, which of course is naturally much lower in the pure government funding variant.

Demand for teachers is logically lowest in the liberal "tuition fee only" vari-ant and highest for pure government funding. Note, however, that the mixed variant "saves" relatively little compared to pure government funding—as far as demand for teachers is concerned it is much closer to the government fund-ing variant than to the liberal variant.

The tuition fee is very sensitive—it is three times lower in the mixed vari-ant, where around half the funding comes from the state and half from tuition fees, than in the liberal "tuition fee only" variant.

Rather surprisingly it turned out that teachers' pay is virtually the same. Hence, the expectations of university lecturers that their pay will rise drasti-cally after the introduction of tuition fees may be very misplaced.

5.3 UNIVERSITY SUPPLY FUNCTION

Let us allow a university operating under the centralist "government subsidy only" variant to charge a tuition fee as well. This will lead to an increase in its supply of study places and to an increase in its probability of survival, i.e. the number of students will increase (the expected number, i.e. the optimum number multiplied by the probability of survival). How much this will be con-straining in terms of optimal (from the university's perspective) filling of the university's capacity is a matter of demand. We model the supply of the university by including the additional tuition fee revenue (compared to the first of the experiments described above).

Figure 29: Supply of the university (expected number of students) the versus tuition fee (mixed variant: the university's revenue includes a government subsidy)

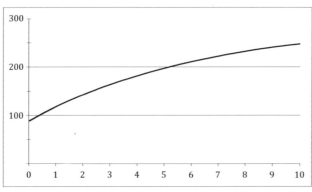

The function is growing and strictly concave. A reduction of the government subsidy would naturally shift the whole curve to the right. The complete abolition of the subsidy would lead to the supply function in Figure 30:

Figure 30: Supply of the university (expected number of students) versus the tuition fee ("no government subsidy" variant)

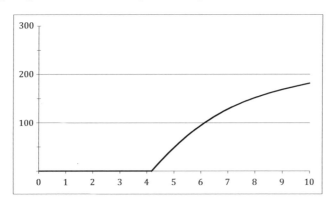

In the mixed variant the university receives a subsidy per student from the donor (the government). For the government subsidy allocation decision it is useful to construct a function showing the number of students (the expected number, i.e. the optimum number multiplied by the survival probability) as a function of the subsidy per student. This is again a supply function, since the subsidy per student in the "government subsidy only" variant represents marginal revenue, i.e. the output price. For the first university in the experiments described above the supply function has the shape depicted in Figure 31.

Figure 31: Supply of the university (expected number of students) versus the subsidy per student ("no tuition fee" variant; subsidy revenue only)

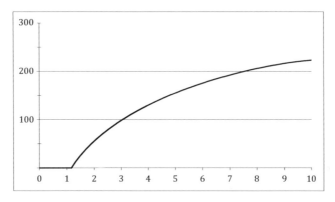

If we take into account neither the average tuition fee nor teachers' pay in the system in the past period, we view the university's supply simply as the product of its capacity and its probability of survival. The supply function is the relation between supply s and marginal revenue MR, i.e. the sum of the tuition fee and the government subsidy per student.

Figure 32: Supply of the university (expected number of students) versus the marginal revenue MR

Like in the standard theory of the firm, therefore, the university supply function is zero up to a certain "price" for its service (the shutdown point) and positive, growing and strictly concave above that point. This holds for the last three supply functions given above (Figures 30, 31, and 32). For the first supply function (Figure 29) the high government subsidy enables the university to survive even with a zero tuition fee, hence this function is positive, growing and strictly concave over its entire domain.

As in the standard theory of the firm, the supply function here describes the subjectively optimal situation (at a particular value of its explanatory variable) of all the situations lying in the set of feasible situations.[64] Taking into account the parameters in the system in the previous period (Figures 29, 30, and 31) puts a stricter constraint on this set of feasible situations by comparison with the last-mentioned supply function (Figure 32), as it is not admissible to deviate from the previous parameters by more than the specified margin. The suitability of using the first or second method to describe supply (i.e. of using the narrower or wider set of feasible situations) will depend on the type of problem being solved.

---

64 The analogy in the theory of the firm is the set of technically feasible situations, i.e. the set of production situations not lying above the production function.

6.

BEHAVIOUR OF A FIRM IN A CENTRALLY PLANNED ECONOMY— THE *HOMO SE ASSECURANS* MODEL

Western economic theory has dealt only marginally with centrally planned economies and has done so by essentially sticking to the standard *homo economicus* paradigm. In our opinion, the views of "insiders" are more interesting and more useful.[65]

The *homo se assecurans*[66] model is a purely microeconomic view of the behaviour of producers in a centrally planned economy. *Homo se assecurans* is an agent maximizing its reserve within a set of production situations that are feasible both technically and according to the plan (i.e. that are both produceable and tolerated by the centre). This is another special case of our general "survival probability maximization" criterion, one which, as we will demonstrate in this chapter, is necessarily anti-efficient in a centrally planned economy.

---

65 See, for example, Kornai, J.: *Economics of Shortage*. Amsterdam: North Holland, 1980, or Mlčoch, L.: Chování československého podnikového sektoru. *VP* No. 384. Praha: Ekonomický ústav ČSAV, 1990, or Brixiová, Z., Bulíř, A.: Output Performance Under Central Planning: A Model of Poor Incentives. *Economic Systems* 27, 1(2003): 27–39, or Hlaváček, J., Kysilka, P., Zieleniec, J.: Plánování a averze k měření. *Politická ekonomie* 36, 5(1988): 593–606.

66 Homo se assecurans = self-insuring man. See Hlaváček, J.: Homo se assecurans. *Politická ekonomie* 35, 6(1987): 633–39.

6.1 SET OF FEASIBLE PRODUCTION SITUATIONS IN A CENTRALLY PLANNED ECONOMY

In contrast to standard microeconomics, the situation in the *homo se asse-curans* model is assessed from two angles, using two utility functions. In addition to the utility of the firm (or its manager/management) the utility of the centre is relevant. The centre imposes its will by defining a plan. Besides the standard microeconomic set of technically feasible production situations $T \equiv \{(y, \vec{x}); y \leq f(\vec{x})\}$ the firm has to "fit" into the production plan set $P \equiv \{(y, \vec{x}); y \geq g(\vec{x})\}$, where $g(\vec{x})$ is the plan function, y is the volume of output produced and $\vec{x} = (x_1, x_2, \ldots, x_n)$ is a vector of inputs (x_i is the volume of the i-th input used). Function $g(\vec{x})$ gives the inefficiency limit tolerated by the centre for each input vector. A company manager who fails to fulfil the plan risks losing his job. The set of feasible production situations is therefore the intersection of the sets $T \cap P$.

The plan function $g(\vec{x})$ is one of the centre's isoquants, i.e. the lines connecting the individual producer's production situations[67] rated equally by the centre. As a utility isoquant, this function must be convex. It is therefore also continuous.

We also assume that the production function $f(\vec{x})$ is strictly concave over its entire domain, i.e. the firm's output exhibits declining marginal product for all its inputs x_1, x_2,..., x_n. Being strictly concave this function is continuous as well.

We will also assume that both functions $f(\vec{x})$ and $g(\vec{x})$ are differentiable. This is a normal assumption in standard microeconomics for both the production function and the utility isoquant.

We will also assume that the plan is implementable, i.e. the intersection of the set of technically feasible production situations T and the set of production situations feasible under the plan P is not empty. For the single-input case, the set of feasible production situations for a producer in a centrally planned economy is illustrated in Figure 33.

---

67   The plan can theoretically have the nature of a single directive (for example, a common lower limit on labour productivity or the profit-to-costs ratio for the whole system). In such case, however, the centre de facto does not attempt to influence—or does not care about—the structure of production in the system. In the opposite case, the centre is forced to issue a firm-specific production plan that takes account of the firm's capacity. This, however, is information which the centre obtains from the producer and which is necessarily subject to interest-based distortions. See Hlaváček, J.: K ekonomické subjektivitě plánovacího centra. *Politická ekonomie* 36, 4(1988): 1039–52.

Figure 33: The set of feasible production situations of a homo se assecurans producer: intersection of the set of technically feasible production situations T and the set of production situations feasible under the plan P

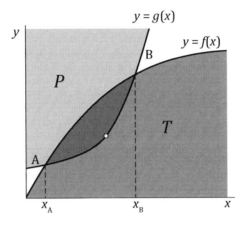

This is a non-empty compact set. The optimum of any continuous function exists in such a set.

6.2 THE INDEX PLANNING METHOD AND THE CRITERION OF A PRODUCER IN A CENTRALLY PLANNED ECONOMY

In a centrally planned economy, the main risk to a manager wishing to keep his job is that of receiving an unimplementable plan for next year.

The company manager does not have a profit motive, as all profit belongs to the state. He is interested solely in keeping his job, which (as we assume[68]) is conditional on implementing the plan. The plan (plan constraint) separates out the production situations which are acceptable to the firm's directly superior economic centre from the set of technically implementable production situations.

However, the supreme master in a communist country is not the economic centre, but the political centre (politburo), which is facing (unsuccessfully, as we now know) the threat of total defeat in economic competition with the West.

---

68 In the real economy, company managers were, for political reasons, sometimes more powerful than centre managers. Changes were then made to the plan ex post. This meant, in fact, a change in the preferences of the planning centre under pressure from the political centre. We abstract from this phenomenon.

The economic centre therefore fulfils the political directive, which (since the 1960s) is primarily to boost production efficiency. However, the economic centre is caught between a rock and a hard place—political pressure from above and evasive manoeuvres by firms from below. Moreover, the firm is in a position of total information superiority vis-à-vis the centre. The only way the centre can produce a balanced and more efficient plan is by means of the "index planning method". This is simple. The status quo (which, of course, is materially balanced) is directly incorporated into the plan for the next period in such a way that either all outputs are multiplied by an index slightly above unity or all inputs are multiplied by an index slightly below unity

Company managers knew all this in advance. Anyone who foolishly revealed his production possibilities by exceeding the previous year's plan would end up with the more difficult—and perhaps impossible—economic problem of fulfilling the plan next year. In the interests of their own survival (in the post of manager) company managers therefore had to set aside reserves (the bigger the better) in order to gain room to implement tougher indexed plans in future years. Moreover, producing well below capacity is less difficult for managers than balancing close to the production-possibility frontier (production function), especially in conditions of uncertainty and general scarcity (shortages of replacement parts, scarcity of foreign exchange to pay for raw materials imports, frequent supply shortfalls, etc.).

So, it wasn't just that producers were not interested in maximizing their profits. It was that they were interested in the exact opposite—in producing as inefficiently as possible and protecting themselves against a tougher future plan by creating the largest possible reserve against it.

6.3 MAXIMIZATION OF THE ABSOLUTE RESERVE

In the original 1980s formulation of the *homo se assecurans* model, the reserve r in production situation $(y, \vec{x})$ (where y is the output volume and $\vec{x}$ is the vector of input volumes) is defined as the difference between the firm's production capacity $f(\vec{x})$ (the value of the production function at point $\vec{x}$) and output volume y, i.e.

$$r = r(y, \vec{x}) = f(\vec{x}) - y .$$

The behaviour of a communist producer was modelled as the maximization of this reserve on the set of feasible production situations, i.e. the constrained maximization problem:

$$\max_{g(\bar{x}) \le y \le f(\bar{x})} r(y, \bar{x}).$$

This model therefore assumes that the utility of the firm is given exclusively by the amount of the reserve, i.e. by the difference between the technically achievable and the actually implemented level of output. The following figure illustrates such utility isoquants for the case of a single input x. The arrow in the figure indicates the direction of increasing utility:

Figure 34: Isoquants of a homo se assecurans producer maximizing its absolute reserve against the plan

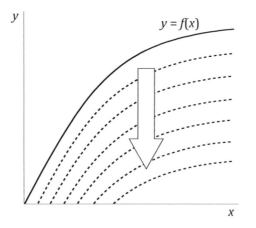

It is noteworthy that the criterion of a *homo se assecurans* producer does not explicitly contain prices. In a centrally planned economy, prices are merely a "language" for formulating the plan constraint.

In Figure 35, which again illustrates the situation for a single (aggregate) input, the production function and the plan function are indicated by unbroken lines and the utility (absolute reserve) isoquants by dotted lines. The tangents to the production and plan functions are drawn with dashed lines. The producer tries to "descend" to the lowest possible isoquant that still allows it to fulfil the plan, i.e. to point E^* with the maximum margin relative to the extinction zone, which for a *homo se assecurans* agent is the set of points (production situations) above the production function line $f(\bar{x})$. The producer's optimal production situation is point $E^* \equiv [x^*, g(x)]$, where x^* is the sole input volume at which the tangents to the two functions $f(x), g(x)$ have the same slope:

Figure 35: The optimal production situation for a producer maximizing its absolute reserve against the technological maximum

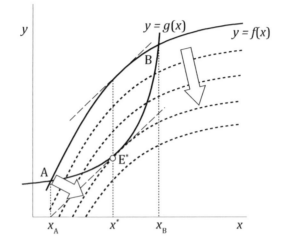

As we explained above, the following assumptions are economically well interpretable:

- strict concavity of $f(\vec{x})$,
- strict convexity of $g(\vec{x})$,
- differentiability of $f(\vec{x})$ and $g(\vec{x})$,
- a non-empty intersection $T \cap P$ of the set of technically feasible production situations T and the set of production situations feasible under the plan P,
- location of the optimal production situation on the plot of the plan function.

As the sum of the strictly concave functions $f(\vec{x})$, $-g(\vec{x})$, the absolute reserve, which, given the final assumption, we can write as $r(y,\vec{x}) = f(\vec{x}) - g(\vec{x})$, is necessarily strictly concave. This means that the problem of maximization of the absolute reserve $r = r(y,\vec{x}) = f(\vec{x}) - y$ on the intersection of the technically feasible set and the set feasible under the plan $T \cap P$ has a unique solution.

The optimal solution (the producer's optimum) is therefore production situation $\left(g(\vec{x}^{*}), \vec{x}^{*} \right)$, where $\vec{x}^{*}$ is the input vector for which the marginal product and the partial derivative of the plan function are equal for all inputs:[69]

$$\left(\frac{\partial f(\vec{x})}{\partial x_i} \right)_{\vec{x}=\vec{x}^{*}} = \left(\frac{\partial g(\vec{x})}{\partial x_i} \right)_{\vec{x}=\vec{x}^{*}} \quad \text{for } i = 1, 2,..., n.$$

---

69 For the proof see Hlaváček, J., Tříska, D.: *Úvod do mikroekonomické analýzy.* Praha: Fakulta sociálních věd UK, 1991, pp. 115–18.

As the optimum necessarily lies on the plot of $g(\vec{x})$, we can express the largest possible absolute reserve with input volume $\vec{x}$ as

$$\tilde{r}(\vec{x}) = r\left(g(\vec{x}^*), \vec{x}^*\right).$$

For the single-input case ($n = 1$), the absolute reserve function under the afore-mentioned assumptions is unimodal and has a unique maximum $x^* \in (x_A, x_B)$, as illustrated in Figure 36[70]:

Figure 36: The maximum absolute reserve against the plan versus input volume: the producer's optimum at point x^*

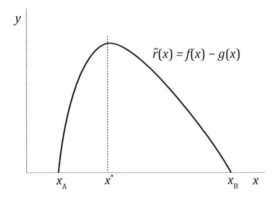

6.4 MAXIMIZATION OF THE RELATIVE RESERVE (I.E. MAXIMIZATION OF THE PARETO PROBABILITY OF SURVIVAL IN A CPE)

One minor shortcoming of the absolute reserve maximization model is that the producer's utility depends solely on the absolute amount of the reserve and not on the volume of production. If a manager has to decide between two firms, he will be more attracted to the one which has the larger reserve-to-production ratio, because in real terms twice the reserve at four times the production volume means half the security against a tightening-up of the plan in terms of percentages, profitability directives[71] and so on. In our opinion, maximization of the relative reserve

---

70   The extreme points x_A, x_B correspond to the identically labelled points in Figure 33.
71   In the early days (the 1950s in Czechoslovakia) the centre was only interested in the volume of produc-tion and firms were stimulated to waste resources on a vast scale. Later on, the centre tried (without success) to reduce such waste.

$$p(y,\vec{x}) = \frac{f(\vec{x}) - y}{f(\vec{x})} = 1 - \frac{y}{f(\vec{x})},$$

as used in all other chapters of this book, is closer to what went on in reality from the early 1960s onwards.

We will stick with the assumptions used in the previous section. As in that section, it is evident that the production situation maximizing the relative reserve lies on the plot of the plan function.

The shape of the producer's utility isoquants is different from that in the previous section. This is illustrated for the single (aggregate) input case by Figure 37 (cf. Figure 34).

Figure 37: Isoquants of a homo se assecurans producer maximizing its relative reserve against the technological maximum

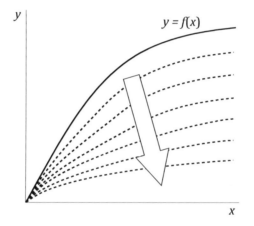

The producer's optimal production situation, illustrated in the following figure, is point $E^{**} \equiv \left(g(x^{**}), x^{**}\right)$, which is the point of contact of the (sole, under the assumptions made) utility isoquant that is tangential to the plan function $g(x)$:

By comparison with the absolute reserve model, a *homo se assecurans* producer maximizing its relative reserve will tend to prefer production situations with lower output volumes:

Whereas the optimal production situation of an absolute reserve-maximizing producer is $E^* \equiv [x^*, g(x^*)]$, where the derivative (the slope of the tangent) at point x^* is the same for both $f(\vec{x})$ and $g(\vec{x})$, the optimal production situation for a relative reserve-maximizing producer is $E^{**} \equiv [x^{**}, g(x^{**})]$, where the logarithmic derivative at point x^{**} is the same for both functions:

$$f'(x^*) = g'(x^*),$$

$$\frac{f'\left(x^{**}\right)}{f\left(x^{**}\right)} = \frac{g'\left(x^{**}\right)}{g\left(x^{**}\right)}.$$

The *homo se assecurans* model (be it with maximization of the absolute reserve or with maximization of the relative reserve) allows us to describe the situation where an economic agent prefers a production situation lying inside the production set. This situation was typical of central planned economies. Standard neoclassical microeconomics with its *homo economicus* paradigm cannot grasp and describe such producer preferences well enough.

The hypothesis of the unreformability of communist-style central planning[72] was based on this model—even instruments that would create pressure for efficiency in a standard economic environment were ineffective or even counterproductive in the *homo se assecurans* environment.[73]

Figure 38: The optimal production situation for a producer maximizing its relative reserve against the plan

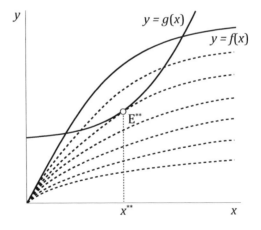

---

72   This hypothesis was formulated and empirically and theoretically tested in Zieleniec, J. et al.: *Česko-slovensko na rozcestí*. Praha: Lidové noviny, 1990, which was based on an extensive research study of the same name conducted at the Economic Institute of the Czechoslovak Academy of Sciences in 1989.

73   For example, "accommodative planning"—part of the "systems of measures to enhance management by planning" introduced in the 1970s—had the opposite effect than intended. See Hlaváček, J.: *Objektivizace informací v plánovacím dialogu—možnosti a meze*. Praha: Academia, 1989, pp. 103–30.

Figure 39: Comparison of a producer maximizing its absolute reserve (optimum E*) with a producer maximizing its relative reserve (optimum E**)

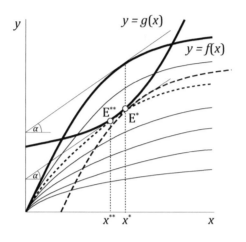

7.

MODEL OF AN ECONOMY WITH WIDESPREAD CORPORATE INSOLVENCY

7.1 THE PROBLEM OF SECONDARY INSOLVENCY

A serious problem which the Czech economy had previously experienced in the early 1990s resurfaced in 2008—"secondary" corporate insolvency.

Secondary insolvency is the situation where a debtor is unable to meet its obligations because one or more of its customers is insolvent. A proportion of debtors become "non-payers", i.e. entities with overdue debts.

The primary cause of the widespread secondary insolvency in the 1990s was the difficult situation of companies privatized by direct methods "on debt". This gave rise to high initial debt levels and also high financial costs.[74]

Late payment of debts was initially tolerated by banks (which is why this period is sometimes referred to as "banking socialism") and by trading partners. To begin with, state-owned banks (i.e. the majority of banks) did not want to hinder the economic transformation process and willingly provided loans even to ailing companies. This ended when loan defaults started to put the banks themselves in danger. In 1993, discretionary constraints on the volume of bank loans were introduced. By then, however, most businesses were insolvent and it was difficult for banks to distinguish between primary and secondary insolvency.

---

74 See Mlčoch, L.: Privatizace bez kapitálu. *Finance a úvěr* 54, 11–12(2004): 560–63.

Another cause of secondary insolvency was poor legislation, which (especially in the early days before a bankruptcy law was adopted[75]) did not give companies enough options to enforce their claims. The strongly monopolistic structure (inherited from the centrally planned economy) also played a role, as companies often had no alternative markets and were dependent on the survival of their sole customer.

The insolvency in the Czech economy in the early 1990s also had macroeconomic causes—declining economic efficiency combined with budget spending cuts in 1993.[76]

The problem of widespread secondary insolvency in the Czech economy re-emerged in 2008.[77] More and more firms got into difficulties paying their debts on time and the volume of overdue debt increased sharply.[78] The cause of this snowball effect was similar to that in the early 1990s—a sudden decrease in banks' willingness to lend (albeit for different reasons—this time fears about the oncoming crisis).[79]

A firm has options to deal with secondary insolvency:

- **insurance with a specialized insurance company** offering bad debt insurance cover. However, there are very few such specialized insurers at present[80] and the low supply is leading to relatively high premiums;
- **a bank bridging loan** to deal with problems caused by unpaid claims. The problem is that the bank will often not grant such credit.[81] Even if it does, the creditor will be left with both a doubtful debt (with high collection costs) and a new loan with the bank;

---

75   See Hlaváček, J., Tůma, Z.: Bankruptcy in the Czech Economy. In *Bankruptcy and the Post-Communist Economies of East Central Europe*, K. Mizsei. New York: Institute for East-West Studies, 1993.

76   See Bulíř, A.: Platební neschopnost: problém "reálné" nebo "peněžní" ekonomiky? *Politická ekonomie* 42, 2(1994): 155–70.

77   See Mertlík, P.: Česku hrozí druhotná platební neschopnost firem. (http://www.radio.cz/cz /clanek/111897 [08-01-2009 07:00 UTC]), or Dvořák, J.: Platit faktury včas se moc nenosí. (http:// www.mesec.cz/clanky/platit-faktury-vcas-se-moc-nenosi/ [15-02-2009 08:11 UTC]).

78   According to Petr Kužel, President of the Czech Chamber of Commerce (see http://www.komora.cz /hk-cr/hlavni-zpravy/art_28565 [16-02-2009 11:20 UTC]), "According to the latest figures claims were up by 40 per cent and past-due claims by as much as 50 per cent at the start of 2009."

79   "Banks bear part of the blame for the current situation. With their restrictive policies and choking of funds for the business sector they are making the situation worse for businesses. It's a vicious circle and there's no escape." (ibid.)

80   At the start of 2009 only four insurers were providing such insurance in the Czech Republic: Atradius, Coface Austria Kreditversicherung, Euler Hermes and Komerční úvěrová pojišťovna EGAP.

81   The government also feels that credit needs to be made more available to SMEs. In February 2009 it increased the bank loan guarantee capacity of the Czech-Moravian Guarantee and Development Bank by CZK 3 billion. This is intended to make banks more willing to lend. For this instrument to be effective, the amount needs to be raised considerably.

- **a change in the VAT payment regime** (as proposed by the Chamber of Commerce in January 2009);
- **discounts** for paying on time.

The third option can be viewed (and has been proposed) as a temporary measure. The first two options are dependent on unrestricted availability of funds both now and in the future. If secondary insolvency keeps growing and banks keep heading for a credit crunch (which will also affect insurance companies), we will be left only with the fourth option, i.e. discounts for paying on time.

As in the 1990s, there will be dual pricing and two types of firms in the economy—"non-payers" and "payers" (firms that duly meet their obligations). Each company will decide what to do with its output, i.e. whether to sell it:

- to non-payers at a higher price (which will boost the company's book profit), or
- to payers at a lower price (which will boost funds available for wages and other immediate payments).

From the microeconomic perspective, in an economy where secondary insolvency is widespread firms are under pressure from two sides: one the one hand they need cash to pay wages and meet other immediate obligations, and on the other hand they are trying to avoid book losses, which could cause the bank to lose patience with overdue loan payments.

The decision on the distribution of output between paying and non-paying customers is therefore a two-criteria problem that is difficult to solve by standard microeconomics in the *homo economicus* paradigm. Our generalized microeconomic model allows us to find a compromise. However, it does not involve vector optimization. There is just one criterion: maximization of the probability of survival, i.e. maximization of the probability of simultaneous avoidance of all risks to the agent's economic survival.

7.2 MODELS OF DECISION-MAKING IN AN ECONOMY WITH WIDESPREAD SECONDARY INSOLVENCY

We will assume that the firm is hit by a large negative demand shock. Besides a reduction in demand, it faces a large deterioration in the solvency of some of its customers. It therefore decides whether to supply to its "unsound" customers (non-payers) and, if yes, at what price. For simplicity, we assume that these non-payers are solvent in the sense that they will pay in the long run, but that they have liquidity problems and are not able to pay immediately. This allows us to abstract from customer credit risk problems. We also assume that the volume of production is already given by the firm's past decisions (for example, its investment or recruitment decisions), hence it is exogenous from the firm's perspective. The costs associated with this production are sunk and cannot be influenced by the firm.

We will use the following notation in the model:

- y volume of production (in natural units),
- y_p production sold to payers,
- y_n production "sold" to non-payers,
- w payroll and other immediate costs,
- c total costs (immediate and non-immediate),
- q the price for payers (the price for non-payers is equal to unity; that is how we define the money unit).

We assume that demand from payers is linear[82]

$$y_p = y \cdot (1-q),$$

i.e. at $q = 1$ (the price charged to non-payers) the firm will sell nothing to payers. If the firm wants to sell its entire output, it must sell part of it to non-payers. We assume that demand from non-payers is unlimited.

The decision-taker knows that it is at risk on the one hand of recording a book loss, i.e. book revenues less than c (immediate and non-immediate costs), and on the other hand of having a shortage of cash, i.e. disposable funds less than w (payroll and other immediate costs).

The decision-taker's problem, therefore, is to split production y between payers and non-payers in such a way as to maximize the probability of avoiding both aforementioned threats:

$$y = y_p + y_n.$$

Given the higher (unit) price charged to non-payers, it is optimal purely in terms of book revenues to sell all output to non-payers (i.e. $q = 1$; maximum profit is equal to $y - c$). On the other hand, maximum cash is generated by price $q = \dfrac{1}{2}$. We will establish this by solving

$$\frac{d}{dq}\left[y_p \cdot q \right] = \frac{d}{dq}\left[y \cdot (1-q) \cdot q \right] = y \cdot (1-2q) = 0.$$

---

82   The assumption of linear demand from payers implicitly entails unrealistic behaviour of payers at very low prices $q \ll \frac{1}{2}$. However, as we will see shortly, the seller will never choose $q < \frac{1}{2}$, as such a large discount would lead counterproductively to a decrease in revenues.

A reduction of the price below $q = \dfrac{1}{2}$ leads both to lower book revenues and to lower disposable funds. The firm therefore necessarily chooses a price in the range of $\dfrac{1}{2} \leq q \leq 1$.

If $\dfrac{1}{2} \leq q < 1$, the firm will gain (relative to $q = 1$) more disposable funds at the cost of lower book revenues. The total reduction in book revenues (and, since output y and costs c are given, the total reduction in book profit as well) resulting from lowering the price for "payers" from $q = 1$ to $q < 1$ is

$$z = y - q \cdot y.(2 - q) = y \cdot (1 - 2q + q^2) = y \cdot (1 - q)^2.$$

Book revenues are given by the difference $y - z$. This is not (as it may seem) a difference between variables in different units, because y is the volume of output in natural units multiplied by the unit price.

We consider the situation where book revenues equal costs to be the boundary of extinction due to low book revenues:

$$y - z = c.$$

According to our assumptions the probability of avoiding the risk associated with low book revenues is proportional to the margin of sales $y - z$ relative to the extinction boundary c:

$$r_1(y,c,q) = \frac{y - z - c}{y - z} = 1 - \frac{c}{y - y \cdot (1 - q)^2}.$$

The amount of output sold to payers (with the aforementioned payer demand function and at price q) is $y_p = y \cdot (1 - q)$. The amount of disposable funds is therefore

$$q \cdot y_p = q \cdot y \cdot (1 - q).$$

We consider the situation where disposable funds equal payroll and other immediate costs $q \cdot y_p = w$ to be the boundary of extinction due to insufficient disposable funds.

The probability of avoiding the risk of insufficient disposable funds is again proportional to the relative margin:

$$r_2(y,q,w) = \frac{q \cdot y \cdot (1 - q) - w}{q \cdot y \cdot (1 - q)} = 1 - \frac{w}{q \cdot y \cdot (1 - q)}.$$

In the following calculations we will assume that the decision-taker has two possible strategies. In the first (so-called "minimax") strategy he identifies the larger of the two risks under consideration and tries to minimize that risk, even at the cost of an increase in the other risk. The second strategy maximizes the probability of simultaneous avoidance of both risks under consideration.[83]

7.2.1 MODEL A: MINIMAX STRATEGY

Let us start by assuming that the decision-taker tries to avoid the larger of these risks, i.e. that his (subjective) feeling of threat is due exclusively to the greater of the two risks under consideration:

$$q^* = \arg\left[\min\left(\max\{F_1(q), F_2(q)\}\right)\right],$$

$$F_1(q) = \frac{w}{q \cdot y \cdot (1-q)},$$

$$F_2(q) = \frac{c}{y - y \cdot (1-q)^2}.$$

Given that a change in price q increases one of these risks and decreases the other, his smallest "minimax" feeling of threat is minimal when the relative margins for the two threats are equal:

$$\frac{w}{q \cdot y \cdot (1-q)} = \frac{c}{y - y \cdot (1-q)^2}.$$

Suppose that the volume of production y is sufficient to avoid extinction due to both reasons under consideration. If this condition is met, and under the aforementioned assumption $c - 2w < 0$, we can rearrange the previous relation to obtain the non-negative optimal price q^* for payers:

---

83 The standard microeconomic approach in the homo economicus paradigm would involve choosing one of the two variables considered here (book revenues and disposable funds) as the variable to be maximized and the other as the constraint defining the set of feasible solutions. The result of this constrained maximization problem would be a situation right on the threat boundary. In the extremely opaque situation of a firm under "banking socialism", this is not realistic—no decision-taker would regard such a risky strategy as optimal.

$$\frac{w}{y\cdot(1-q)}=\frac{c}{y-y\cdot(1-q)^2}=\frac{c}{y-y+2q\cdot y-q^2\cdot y}=\frac{c}{y\cdot q\cdot(2-q)},$$

$$\frac{w}{1-q}=\frac{c}{q\cdot(2-q)},$$

$$0\le q^*=\frac{c-2w}{c-w}<1.$$

The firm then splits the sale of its output as follows:

$$y_p=y\cdot(1-q)=y\cdot\frac{w}{c-w},$$

$$y_n=y-y\cdot\frac{w}{c-w}=y\cdot\frac{c-2w}{c-w}.$$

The share of production "sold" to non-payers in total production is characteristic of the degree of secondary insolvency. Under the assumptions adopted, the following holds for this share:

$$v(c,v)=\frac{y_n}{y_n+y_p}=\frac{c-2w}{w+c-2w}=\frac{c-2w}{c-w}.$$

The proportion of production sold to payers is therefore given by the share of immediate costs in total costs:

$$1-v(c,v)=\frac{w}{c-w}.$$

In other words, decision-takers maximizing the probability of their own survival will set a reduced price for payers q^* in such a way that the division of their production between payers and non-payers "copies" the ratio of their immediate costs to their non-immediate costs. Consequently, all agents—both strongly threatened and less strongly threatened—will adopt the practice of declaring secondary insolvency. This does not mean, however, that all agents will behave identically. Higher secondary insolvency will (in the logic of this model) be recorded by firms with a higher proportion of immediate (especially payroll) costs.

7.2.2 MODEL B: MINIMUM EXTINCTION RISK STRATEGY

According to the assumptions made above for the probability of avoidance of the two risks under consideration, it holds that

$$q^* = \arg\left[\min\left(F_1(y,c,q)+F_2(y,c,q)\right)-\left(F_1(y,c,q)\cdot F_2(y,c,q)\right)\right],$$

$$F_1(q)=\frac{w}{q\cdot y\cdot(1-q)},$$

$$F_2(q)=\frac{c}{y-y\cdot(1-q)^2}.$$

At the optimum $q = q^*$ (for the optimal price reduction for "payers"), for the value of distribution function F and the value of probability density function f it holds that

$$F_1'(q)+F_2'(q)-\left(F_1(q)\cdot F_2(q)\right)'=0,$$

$$F_1'(q)\cdot(1-F_2(q))=F_2'(q)\cdot(1-F_1(q)),$$

$$\frac{F_1'(q)}{F_2'(q)}=\frac{1-F_1(q)}{1-F_2(q)}=\frac{f_1(q)}{f_2(q)}.$$

The solution of this non-trivial equation depends, of course, on the relationship between parameters y, c and w. If the values of distribution functions $F_1(q)$ and $F_2(q)$ are close, the optimal strategy will be similar to the "minimax" strategy described above. If $F_1(q) >> F_2(q)$, the "bottleneck" is the constraint relating to disposable funds and the optimal price q^* will be lower (i.e. the discount for payers will be bigger). If $F_1(q) << F_2(q)$, the "bottleneck" is accounting profit and price q^* will be close to unity (corresponding to a zero discount).

We will denote by k the ratio of total costs to revenues at the maximum unit price:

$$c = y\cdot k.$$

Furthermore, we will denote by m the ratio of immediate costs to total costs:

$$w = c\cdot m = y\cdot k\cdot m.$$

By substituting into the above equations we obtain:

$$F_1(q) = \frac{k \cdot m}{q \cdot (1-q)},$$

$$F_2(q) = \frac{k}{q \cdot (2-q)}.$$

We obtain the optimal price for payers q (i.e. the price maximizing the decision-taker's probability of survival) by solving the equation:

$$F_1'(q) \cdot (1 - F_2(q)) = F_2'(q) \cdot (1 - F_1(q)).$$ (*)

Let us calculate the derivative and substitute into (*):

$$F_1'(q) = k \cdot m \cdot \frac{2q-1}{q^2 \cdot (1-q)^2},$$

$$F_2'(q) = 2 \cdot k \cdot \frac{1-q}{q^2 \cdot (2-q)^2},$$

$$F_1'(q) \cdot (1 - F_2(q)) = k \cdot m \cdot \frac{2q-1}{q^2 \cdot (1-q)^2} \cdot \frac{q \cdot (2-q) - k}{q \cdot (2-q)},$$

$$F_2'(q) \cdot (1 - F_1(q)) = 2 \cdot k \cdot \frac{1-q}{q^2 \cdot (2-q)^2} \cdot \frac{q \cdot (1-q) - k \cdot m}{q \cdot (1-q)},$$

so the optimum condition is

$$k \cdot m \cdot \frac{2q-1}{q^2 \cdot (1-q)^2} \cdot \frac{q \cdot (2-q) - k}{q \cdot (2-q)} = 2 \cdot k \cdot \frac{1-q}{q^2 \cdot (2-q)^2} \cdot \frac{q \cdot (1-q) - k \cdot m}{q \cdot (1-q)}.$$

After rearranging we obtain:

$$m \cdot (2q-1) \cdot (2-q) \cdot (q \cdot (2-q) - k) - 2 \cdot (1-q)^2 \cdot (q \cdot (1-q) - k \cdot m) = 0.$$

We have solved this equation numerically for various values of k and m. The results are summarized in the following table:

Table 7: Optimal price for payers in relation to the ratio of total and immediate costs to production

	m = 0.9	m = 0.8	m = 0.7	m = 0.6	m = 0.5	m = 0.4	m = 0.3	m = 0.2	m = 0.1
k = 0.95	0.5	0.5	0.5	0.5	0.5	0.5	0.5	0.77	0.85
k = 0.9	0.5	0.5	0.5	0.5	0.5	0.5	0.5	0.73	0.81
k = 0.8	0.5	0.5	0.5	0.5	0.5	0.5	0.58	0.7	0.78
k = 0.7	0.5	0.5	0.5	0.5	0.5	0.5	0.6	0.68	0.75
k = 0.6	0.5	0.5	0.5	0.5	0.5	0.53	0.6	0.66	0.74
k = 0.5	0.5	0.5	0.5	0.5	0.5	0.56	0.61	0.66	0.73
k = 0.4	0.5	0.5	0.5	0.51	0.54	0.57	0.61	0.65	0.71
k = 0.3	0.5	0.51	0.52	0.54	0.56	0.58	0.61	0.65	0.71
k = 0.2	0.53	0.53	0.54	0.55	0.57	0.59	0.61	0.64	0.7
k = 0.1	0.54	0.55	0.56	0.56	0.58	0.59	0.61	0.64	0.69

Source: Authors' calculations

The greater is the risk stemming from insufficient disposable funds, the more sellers will reduce the price for payers. However, they will not reduce it below the level that maximizes the amount of disposable funds acquired, i.e. below $q = 0.5$. For practically all combinations of k and m our model producer also appeals to non-payers. If the ratio of immediate costs is low (as is the case in the last four columns of the table), the producer is not forced to offer the maximum discount.

*   *   *

Economically non-standard environments do not rule out rational (albeit non-standard from the perspective of the *homo economicus* paradigm) economic decision-making. The methodology of generalized microeconomics allows us to model and microeconomically analyse such decision-making.

8.

THE PRODUCER'S OPTIMUM UNDER INCREASING RETURNS TO SCALE

In the current economy we are observing an unprecedented phenomenon. For some technologies (e.g. those facilitating the provision and intermediation of information) a firm will pay high fixed costs (and potentially overcome other barriers to entry to the market). Subsequently, however, practically any increase in the volume of services it provides (due, for example, to a growing customer base) will increase its revenue, while its costs increase only slightly, if at all. In such case, its marginal costs are zero and its returns to scale as output increases are increasing over the entire domain of the production function (contrary to the assumption of decreasing returns to scale made in standard microeconomics).

Standard neoclassical microeconomics does not concern itself too much with this situation. For a viable technology with increasing returns to scale the optimal volume of production (in the sense of maximum profitability) tends to infinity in conditions of increasing returns to scale with given prices. In a monopoly situation, the optimal production volume is q^*, at which marginal revenue is equal to (in this case zero) marginal costs $MC = 0$. The optimal price p^* and the optimal production volume q^* are both given by the demand function $D(p)$ and marginal revenue $MR(q)$, which can be derived from the demand function. Profit is maximized at the output volume at which marginal revenue equals marginal costs. Figure 40 illustrates this for a linear demand function.

Figure 40: The monopolist's optimum E given zero marginal costs in standard microeconomics

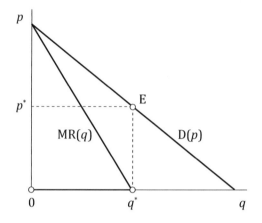

A different situation arises if the monopolist is threatened by the entry of a competitor hitherto deterred by the high fixed costs. This is not directly a standard game situation—the "opponent" is merely a suspected possibility. The threshold price (profitability) that attracts the competitor is unknown to the decision-taker. It involves a sort of choice under uncertainty.[84]

Standard economics does not take into account the risks associated with the potential entry of an unknown competitor into a monopoly industry and the related aversion to situations with a high degree of such risk in a producer's decisions. Yet risk aversion and aversion to the unknown are among the most important characteristics of people's choices in the theory of human motivation (self-actualization).[85]

In standard economic models, risk aversion is modelled on the basis of a strictly concave function of the expected utility of income[86] or by considering the size of the perceived loss in relation to the risk by applying a criterion in the form of a weighted average of the expected value and the variance, referred to

84 The issue of choice when the price is unknown is studied mainly in consumer theory (see, for example, the review article McMillan, J., Rothschild, M.: Searching for the Lowest Price when the Distribution of Prices is Unknown. *Journal of Political Economy* 82, 4(1974), 689–711, but also in general microeconomics (see, for example, Newbery, D. M. G., Stiglitz, J. E.: *The Theory of Commodity Price Stabilization: A Study in the Economics of Risk*. Oxford: Oxford University Press, 1981). For general information on this area of microeconomics see also Gravelle, H., Rees, R.: *Microeconomics*. London: Longman, 1992.

85 See, for example, Maslow, A. H.: *Motivation and Personality*. New York: Harper and Row, 1970, or Hlaváček, J. et al.: *Mikroekonomie sounáležitosti se společenstvím*. Praha: Karolinum, 1999, section 2.1.

86 The Arrow-Pratt measure of local risk aversion is defined as $r(d) = -u''(d)/u'(d)$, where d is income and u is expected utility. The Arrow-Pratt measure of relative risk aversion is defined as $\rho(d) = -d \cdot u''(d)/u'(d)$. See Varian, H. R.: *Microeconomic Analysis*. New York: W. W. Norton, 1992.

as mean-variance utility (ibid.). Another possibility is the stochastic approach to understanding risk.[87]

We assume that firms have the option of entering the industry. However, this entry is not cost-free but is conditional on payment of a high entrance fee (taking the form of fixed costs). The producer in our model operates in conditions of increasing returns to scale and zero marginal costs. It does not try to maximize its instantaneous profit, as an extremely high profit might attract another agent able and willing to pay the entrance fee.

If a high price or high profit does attract a competitor, the firm's revenue will fall dramatically. Let us assume that a second agent will enter when the price exceeds p_h, namely the threshold price at which it pays the second agent to pay the high entry costs. We will also assume that even after the second agent enters the market, the incumbent monopolist will continue (at least temporarily) to have a price-setting advantage over the newly arrived producer. This means that the new competitor will set the same price as the incumbent monopolist.[88] Let us assume that the total quantity demanded $D(p)$ will be split equally between the two oligopolists, so the demand of the decision-taker $d(p)$ is halved if a competitor enters the market (i.e. $d(p) = D(p)/2$ for $p > p_h$) and is equal to total demand in the opposite case (i.e. $d(p) = D(p)$ for $p \le p_h$). The slope of the marginal revenue curve will be one-quarter of the slope of the total demand curve $D(p)$ for $p > p_h$ and just one-half for $p \le p_h$.

Figure 41: Threat of entry of a second agent: individual demand $d(p)$ and marginal revenue MR(q)

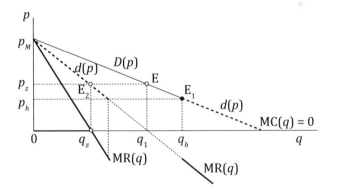

87   See, for example, Stiglitz, J.: Incentives, Risk and Information: Notes Toward a Theory of Hierarchy. *Bell Journal of Economics* 6, 2(1975): 552–79, or Diamond, P., Stiglitz, J. E.: Increases in Risk and Risk Aversion. *Journal of Economic Theory* 8, 3(1974): 337–60. For an empirical analysis of risk aversion, see Applebaum, E., Katz, E.: Measures of Risk Aversion and Comparative Statics of Industry Equilibrium. *American Economic Review* 76, 3(1986): 524–29.

88   This is the "leader–follower" relationship from the Stackelberg model applied to price-setting. See Gravelle, H., Rees, R.: *Microeconomics*. London: Longman, 1992.

Point E, which is the optimum in the standard approach (Figure 41), is not a feasible solution here. Point E_1 at price p_h and point E_2 at price $p_z > p_h$ come into consideration for the choice. However, our firm (i.e. the firm whose choice we are modelling) does not know the threshold price p_h and is threatened with a sudden drop in output combined with a fatal decrease in profitability.

The profit function (the relation between profit Π and output price p) has the shape depicted in Figure 42. It is discontinuous and has two local maxima—at price p_h and at price p_z. These local maxima correspond to points E_1 and E_2 in Figure 41. Because we assume a threat due to the entry of a competitor, it is sensible to count on the local maximum at price p_z being less profitable (if at all). This is because it represents a substantially lower number of customers, since the considerable decrease in the volume of output is associated with a significant increase in average costs.

Figure 42: The profit function $\Pi(p)$, discontinuous at point p_h

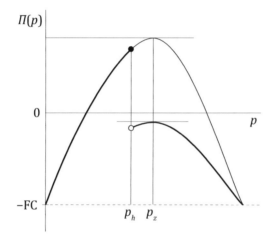

If, therefore, the firm knows the marginal price for the entry of the second agent p_h (a competitor will enter the market when this price is exceeded), the optimal (profit-maximizing) strategy is to choose this marginal price p_h with output volume q_h (i.e. point E_1 in Figure 41). The optimal pricing strategy in this case balances on the very margin of survival. If, though, a firm "with a self-preservation instinct" does not have such information, it will not try to get even close to price $p = p_h$, because it would face a high risk of extinction. However, it will not choose the local profit maximum at price p_z (point E_2 in Figure 41) either, because that is a loss situation.

So, what pricing strategy does the firm prefer in this situation? It is reasonable to expect the decision-taker to choose the strategy it regards as optimal from the point of view of the firm's probability of survival.[89] In this case, the firm tries to avoid risky situations and has a tendency to pull back from its extinction zone. Figure 43 illustrates the extinction zone Ψ. The area below the horizontal axis represents extinction due to low profitability, while the area to the right of the $p = p_h$ line represents the entry of competitors attracted by the high price.

Figure 43: Extinction zone $\Psi \equiv \{(p, \pi); (\Pi < 0) \vee (p > p_h)\}$

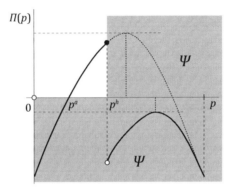

The optimal price will lie somewhere within the open interval (p_a, p_h). Let us assume that the two threats (entry of competitor and low profit) are independent. We will denote the probability of extinction at output price p by $\eta_1(p), \eta_2(p)$, where $\eta_1(p)$ relates to the threat of ruinous entry of competition and $\eta_2(p)$ is the probability of extinction due to profit falling below zero.

8.1 MODEL A: UNIFORM DISTRIBUTIONS OF THE PROBABILITY OF EXTINCTION W.R.T. PRICE

In sections 8.1 and 8.2 we assume for simplicity uniform distributions of the probability of extinction with respect to price p, i.e. distribution functions in the form

$$\eta_1(p) = \frac{p - p_0}{p_h - p_0} \qquad \text{in the interval } \langle p_0, p_h \rangle,$$

$$= 0 \qquad \text{for } p < p_0,$$

$$= 1 \qquad \text{for } p > p_h,$$

89 The general formulation of the producer's decision-making model in conditions of multiple threats is given in Hlaváček, J. et al.: *Mikroekonomie sounáležitosti se společenstvím*. Praha: Karolinum, 1999, pp. 100–11.

where p_0 is the price at which the possibility of competitors entering vanishes entirely and p_h is the lowest price that induces competitors to enter, and

$$\eta_2(p) = \frac{p_2 - p}{p_2 - p_1} \qquad \text{in the interval } \langle p_1, p_2 \rangle,$$

$$= 1 \qquad \text{for } p < p_1,$$
$$= 0 \qquad \text{for } p > p_2,$$

where p_2 is the lowest price at which the risk of extinction due to insufficient profit vanishes entirely. The firm will certainly pay for insufficient profit with extinction for $p < p_1 < p_h$.

The following two figures show the probability distribution functions for these distributions:

Figure 44: The probability of extinction $\eta_1(p)$ due to entry of competition at price p

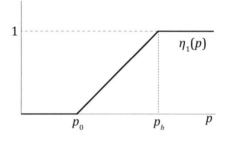

Figure 45: The probability of extinction $\eta_2(p)$ due to low profit at price p

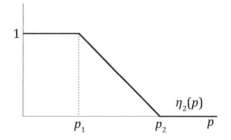

The probability of survival in this model is maximized by the price p^* at which the following function reaches a maximum:

$$\eta_A(p) = [1 - \eta_1(p)] \cdot [1 - \eta_2(p)] = K \cdot (p_h - p) \cdot (p - p_1),$$

$$K = \frac{1}{(p_h - p_2) \cdot (p_2 - p_1)}.$$

For the derivative of function $\eta(p)$ it holds that

$$\eta'_A(p) = K \cdot (p_h + p_1 - 2p).$$

If we set $\eta'_A(p) = 0$, we get the following for the argument of the maximum[90]:

$$p^* = \frac{p_h + p_1}{2}.$$

Here, not surprisingly, the optimal price is the average of the price levels at which the threat of extinction due to one of the two reasons under consideration materializes with 100% certainty.

8.2 MODEL B: UNIFORM DISTRIBUTIONS OF THE PROBABILITY OF EXTINCTION W.R.T. PROFITABILITY

Now let us assume, more realistically, uniform distributions of the probability

of extinction with respect to profitability $\pi = \dfrac{\Pi}{FC}$. We will denote

$\pi_h = \pi(p_h)$,

$\pi_j = \pi(p_j)$ for $j = 1, 2$.

We assume here extinction distribution functions in the form:

$$\eta_1(\pi) = \frac{\pi - \pi_0}{\pi_h - \pi_0} \qquad \text{in the interval } \langle p_0, p_h \rangle,$$

$$= 0 \qquad \text{for } \pi < \pi_0,$$
$$= 1 \qquad \text{for } \pi > \pi_h,$$

where π_0 is the profitability level at which the possibility of competitors enter-

ing vanishes entirely, π_h is the lowest profitability level $\pi = \dfrac{\Pi}{FC}$ that induces competitors to enter with 100% probability, and similarly

---

90 This is a maximum because $\lambda''(p) = -2K < 0$ for all p and hence for p^* as well.

$$\eta_2(\pi) = \frac{\pi_2 - \pi}{\pi_2 - \pi_1} \qquad \text{in the interval } \langle \pi_1, \pi_2 \rangle,$$

$$= 1 \qquad \text{for } \pi < \pi_1,$$
$$= 0 \qquad \text{for } \pi > \pi_2,$$

where π_2 is the lowest profitability at which the risk of extinction due to insufficient profit vanishes entirely. The firm will certainly pay for insufficient profit with extinction for $\pi \leq \pi_1$.

The probability of survival in this model is maximized by the profitability π^* at which the following survival probability function reaches a maximum:

$$\eta_B(\pi) = K \cdot \left[1 - \eta_1(\pi)\right] \cdot \left[1 - \eta_2(\pi)\right],$$

$$K = \frac{1}{\left(\pi_h - \pi_0\right) \cdot \left(\pi_2 - \pi_1\right)},$$

$$\pi = \frac{\Pi}{FC} = \frac{p \cdot D(p) - FC}{FC}.$$

Plots 1 and 2 in Figure 46 represent the distribution functions of the uniform distribution of the risk of extinction $\eta_1(\pi)$, $\eta_2(\pi)$ and plot 3 is the probability of survival $\eta_B(\pi)$. The optimal profitability for uniform distributions of the risk of extinction is at point π^*.

Analogously to the previous section, if we set $\eta'_B(p) = 0$, we get the following for the argument of the maximum of the probability of survival:

$$\pi^* = \frac{\pi_h + \pi_1}{2}.$$

Hence, the optimal price p^* must fulfil the condition

$$p_h \cdot D(p_h) + p_1 \cdot D(p_1) = 2 \cdot p^* \cdot D(p^*)$$

It therefore holds that the survival-probability-maximizing price p^* lies in the interval $(\min(p_h, p_1); \max(p_h, p_1))$ and does not depend on the other parameters of the model.

Figure 46: The probability of survival and optimal profitability for uniform distributions of the risk of extinction

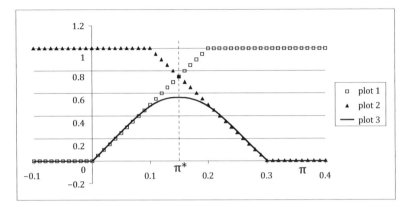

8.3 MODEL C: NORMAL DISTRIBUTIONS OF THE PROBABILITY OF EXTINCTION W.R.T. PROFITABILITY

In this model we will work with the normal distribution of the probability of extinction due to the two reasons under consideration with respect to profitability $\pi = \dfrac{\Pi}{FC}$. As it is not generally possible to determine the cumulative distribution function of the normal distribution algebraically, we will use estimates obtained by numerical methods for our subsequent conclusions.

In this model we are looking for the profitability π^* at which the following survival probability function reaches a maximum

$$\eta(\pi) = K \cdot [1 - \eta_1(\pi)] \cdot [1 - \eta_2(\pi)], \text{ where}$$

$$K = \frac{1}{\left(\pi_h - \pi_0\right) \cdot \left(\pi_2 - \pi_1\right)},$$

$$\pi = \frac{\Pi}{FC} = \frac{p \cdot D(p) - FC}{FC}.$$

The optimal profitability π^* is the root of equation $\Omega(\pi) = 0$, where

$$\Omega(\pi) = f_1(\pi) - f_1(\pi) \cdot \Phi_2(\pi) - f_2(\pi) \cdot \Phi_1(\pi).$$

The symbols used have the following meanings:

f_j the density of the distribution of the probability of extinction due to the j-th reason ($j = 1, 2$),

Φ_j the cumulative distribution function of the probability of survival (i.e. the probability of avoidance of extinction due to $j = 1, 2$),

$\Omega(\pi)$ the derivative (with respect to profit) of the agent's probability of survival (i.e. the probability of avoidance of both threats).

Figure 47: The probability of survival and optimal profitability for normal distributions of the risk of extinction

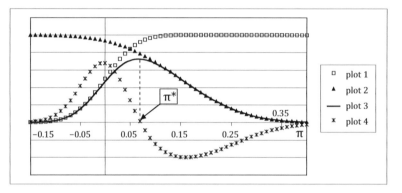

Plots 1 and 2 in Figure 47 represent the distribution functions of the probability of extinction due to $j = 1, 2$, plot 3 is the firm's probability of survival (i.e. the probability of avoidance of both threats of extinction) $\eta(\pi)$, and plot 4 represents function $\Omega(\pi)$. The location of the optimum is π^*.

Figures 48 and 49 show the plot of the probability of survival (i.e. the probability of avoidance of both threats of extinction) against profitability π and the magnitude of the optimal profitability π^* for the case where the two distributions have the same standard deviation. In this case, the maximum probability of survival occurs for the profitability which corresponds to the average of the means of the two distributions and which does not depend on the other parameters of the model (the common size of the variance and the slope of the demand function).

Figure 48 assumes normal distributions of the risk of extinction $N_1(a_1 = 0; \sigma_1 = 0.1)$, $N_2(a_2 = 0.2; \sigma_2 = 0.1)$. Plots 1 and 2 are the probabilities of extinction due to $j = 1, 2$ (see Figures 44 and 45) and plot 3 is the dependence of the agent's probability of survival on profit π.

Figure 49 assumes normal distributions of the risk of extinction $N_1(a_1 = 0; \sigma_1 = 0.2)$, $N_2(a_2 = 0,3; \sigma_2 = 0.2)$. Plot 3 represents the probability of survival $\lambda(\pi)$ and the optimal profitability is π^*.

Figure 48: The probability of survival and optimal profitability π^* for normal distributions of the risk of extinction for the same standard deviations $\sigma_1 = \sigma_2 = 0.1$

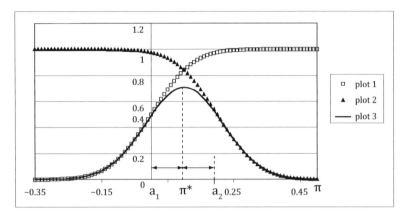

Figure 49: Ditto for $\sigma_1 = \sigma_2 = 0.2$

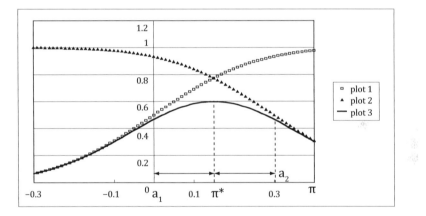

Figures 50 and 51 illustrate the case where the variances of the extinction probability distributions with respect to the chosen profitability differ significantly. In both figures, plot 3 represents the agent's probability of survival and plots 1 and 2 the probabilities of extinction due to one of the reasons under consideration. The optimal profitability is again π^*. In the first case, the variance of the probability of extinction due to the entry of another competitor is the lower: $N_1(a_1 = 0; \sigma_1 = 0.05)$, $N_2(a_2 = 0.2; \sigma_2 = 0.4)$. In the second case, described in Figure 45, the variance of the probability of extinction due to insufficient profit is the lower: $N_1(a_1 = 0; \sigma_1 = 0.4)$, $N_2(a_2 = 0.2; \sigma_2 = 0.05)$. In both cases, the optimal profit level π^* moves from the average of the means of the two distributions towards the mean of the distribution with the higher variance.

Figure 50: The probability of survival and optimal profitability π^* for normal distributions of the risk of extinction for different standard deviations $\sigma_1 < \sigma_2$

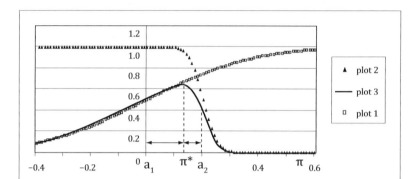

Figure 51: Ditto for $\sigma_1 > \sigma_2$

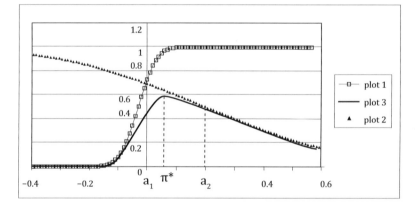

It is clear that the main determinants of the size of the optimal profit are the means of the two distributions and the relationship between their variances. If we fix the means (say at 0 and 2) we can compare the size of the optimal profit as a function of the variances.

When the two variances are the same, the optimal profitability will be close to the average of the two means, i.e. to the diagonal of the square in Figure 52. For small positive variances of both distributions ($\sigma_1 < 0.25$ and $\sigma_2 < 0.25$) the optimal profitability will also be close to the average of the two means. The agent's behaviour changes only when the variances of the probabilities of extinction due to the two reasons differ significantly and are not very low (i.e. are greater than 0.25).

It can be shown[91] that when one of the variances is fixed at a constant value and when the other one is increased, the optimal probability of survival remains constant up to a certain threshold representing a qualitative change. Beyond this threshold the optimal profitability starts to change relatively significantly.

Figure 52: Optimal profit as a function of the variances of the random distribution of the two threats under consideration

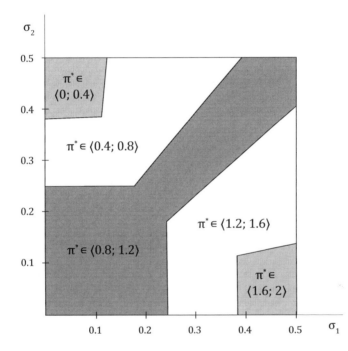

We have successfully investigated the problem of the firm's optimal business strategy in conditions of increasing returns to scale given high initial fixed costs of entry into the market and zero marginal costs where the firm is threatened by extinction due to both low profitability and ruinous entry of a competitor. The optimum strategy is a compromise (between the two threats) that involves choosing the price at which the rise in price is associated with an equal fall and rise, respectively, in the probabilities of extinction due to the two reasons (low profit and entry of a competitor). It turns out that this problem has a single solution (with both uniform and normal distributions of the probabilities of

91 See Hlaváček, J., Hlaváček, M.: Optimum výrobce při stále rostoucích výnosech z rozsahu. *Politická ekonomie* 50, 5(2002): 689–98.

extinction). This allows us to construct a supply function. Where the sole threat to the firm is low profitability, this function is coincident with the standard supply function of a monopoly producer. The described approach is therefore obviously again a generalization (and not a refutation) of the standard micro-economic approach. Where both extinction threats are active, the location of the optimum depends also on the relationship between the variances of the probability of extinction. If the variances are identical, the optimal profit is at the level of the arithmetic average of the means of the two distributions. If one of the variances increases in relation to the other, the optimal profit level shifts towards the mean of the distribution having the lower variance, although only when the variance exceeds a certain level. From this we can conclude that under certain conditions (a high and non-uniform degree of uncertainty regarding the various threat factors) there is a risk that a relatively minor increase in uncertainty in a system will result in a qualitative change in the behaviour of the system and its sensitivity to changes in its parameters. This represents a potential element of instability in markets of the type under analysis.

9.

MODELS OF MARKET ALLOCATION OF EXTERNALITIES, GENERALIZED COASE THEOREM

9.1 EMISSIONS PERMIT MARKET

The worsening climate forced the UN to adopt the Framework Convention on Climate Change in 1992. The Kyoto Protocol was annexed to this Convention in 1997. Under the Protocol, the world's industrial countries committed themselves to reducing emissions of greenhouse gases by 5.2% compared to the 1990 level by the year 2012. Cutting emissions of greenhouse gases should, according to the Protocol, slow the pace of climate change and global warming. The Czech Republic ratified the Kyoto Protocol in 2001.

One of the main tools for reducing pollution is emissions trading. This system—consisting of Joint Implementation (JI) and the Clean Development Mechanism (CDM)—provides economic agents with market-based incentives to cut emissions of pollutants. The system also makes it possible for the state to intervene effectively to reduce carbon dioxide emissions, for example. The state issues permits only for the number of tonnes of greenhouse gas emissions it wishes to allow. In the Czech Republic, this amount is set in a National Allocation Plan.

Firms can trade the permits they do not use. The permits therefore function similarly to securities. They can be sold to other polluters who cannot keep within the limits.[92]

---

92 For instance, the biggest Czech polluter, the power company ČEZ, earned more than a billion Czech crowns in this way in 2007. However, firms are not required to sell their permits within any time-limit. In 2007, for example, the market price of permits fell and many businesses held them speculatively in expectation of a rise in the market price.

It is believed that this system will contribute to the allocation of environmental investments to areas of maximum effect and therefore reduce emissions overall.

Another stated advantage of the emissions trading system is that it enables resources to be pooled for environmental investments that a single firm would otherwise find very difficult to carry out.

In this section we will try to model the behaviour of an agent that is trying to avoid two risks: the risk of exceeding the emissions limit, and the risk of insolvency due to low profitability. The agent can reduce one of these risks at the expense of the other by buying or selling emissions permits.

We will use the following notation in the model:

Y is output of a firm,

q is the price of the product,

π is profit per unit of output,

b is the boundary of the zone of the threat due to low profitability,

G is the volume of emissions,

γ is emissions per unit of output,

G_0 is the initial number of emissions permits,

ω is the market price of a permit,

ζ is the number of permits bought (with $\zeta < 0$ sold).

The Pareto probability of extinction due to low profitability is

$$p_1(\xi) = 1 - \frac{b}{\pi \cdot Y - \zeta \cdot \omega}.$$

We assume that the firm is not allowed to exceed the emissions limit given by the number of permits it holds, i.e. there is a prohibitive penalty for exceeding this limit. The probability of extinction due to this reason is

$$p_2(\xi) = 1 - \frac{G_0}{\gamma \cdot Y + \zeta \cdot \omega}.$$

The firm maximizes its probability of survival

$$p(\xi) = p_1(\xi) \cdot p_2(\xi) = \frac{\Pi_0 \cdot b}{(\pi \cdot Y - \zeta \cdot \omega) \cdot (\gamma \cdot Y + \zeta \cdot \omega)}.$$

Because the sum of the factors in the denominator is constant (and because a square has a larger area than any other rectangle with the same perimeter) it holds that the probability of survival is maximized by the sale of emissions permits ζ^* at which the factors in the denominator are equal:

$$\pi \cdot Y - \zeta^* \cdot \omega = \gamma \cdot Y + \zeta^* \cdot \omega.$$

The optimum (survival-probability-maximizing) number of permits is therefore

$$\zeta^* = \frac{Y}{2 \cdot \omega} \cdot (\pi - \gamma).$$

If $\zeta^* > G_0$, the firm will buy $\zeta^* - G_0$ permits. If, by contrast, $\zeta^* < G_0$, the firm will sell $\zeta^* - G_0$ permits.

The standard market mechanism will then deliver the emissions permit price ω^* at which the number of permits demanded and supplied is equal, i.e. at which the following relation holds (where i is the index of the agent):

$$\sum_i \zeta^*_i (\omega^*) = 0.$$

Under the stated (essentially realistic) assumptions the demand and supply functions of market agents are smooth functions and the equilibrium price ω^* certainly exists and is unique, because with rising price ω both demand (the sum of positive $\zeta^*_i(\omega)$) and supply (the sum of negative $\zeta^*_i(\omega)$) for permits changes continuously and the gap between supply and demand on the emissions market is an increasing function of the permit price.

9.2 THE COASE THEOREM FOR NEGATIVE EXTERNALITIES

Allowing injuring and injured parties to negotiate compensation for a negative externality generates an efficient outcome (assuming negligible bargaining costs[93]) regardless, in a sense (see below), of the legal regime.

---

93   The assumption of zero (negligible) transaction costs makes the Coase theorem applicable only to situations with a relatively small number of parties, since the number of possible combinations of actors of the interaction between the parties is subject to the "curse of dimensionality". If the number of parties is 10, the number of subsets created from this set of parties is less than 1000, and for $n = 15$ it exceeds 32,000. But for $n = 20$ there are more than 7 million "combinations" of parties to the Coase negotiation process. The transaction costs therefore exceed the positive effect of bargaining and the conclusion that bargaining is efficient no longer applies.

The classic example used in Coase's landmark paper[94] is that of a doctor disturbed in his work by noise caused by the machinery of a confectioner in a neighbouring building. The traditional economic opinion was restrictive: the noise is harming the doctor, so the confectioner is obliged to eliminate the source of the noise. Coase noticed a seemingly obvious fact: eliminating the source of noise might help the doctor, but it will harm the confectioner. Either way, someone will always suffer damage. From the overall perspective it would clearly be better to implement the option involving less damage. Coase added that if we allow bargaining between the injured party and the "guilty party", it is advantageous to both parties to implement the option involving the less serious harm.

In other words, when the theorem's assumptions are satisfied, negotiations between the parties will always lead to bargains that are advantageous to all the parties and simultaneously to optimal allocation of resources to environmental investments. Producers will, in their own interest in the given conditions, achieve what the state is trying in vain to achieve owing to a shortage of information. The negative externality will reach a level that is optimal from the point of view of society, for example from the point of view of a common owner of two factories.

In the following section we will formulate the standard Coase theorem for the most common case of a negative externality affecting two producers.

9.2.1 THE COASE THEOREM FOR NEGATIVE EXTERNALITIES: THE CASE OF TWO PRODUCERS

We solve the problem of two producers (a polluter and an injured party). We assume zero (negligible) costs associated with negotiating compensation.

We use the following notation:

x is the amount of pollution,

$\Pi(x)$ is the polluter's profit at the level of activity causing pollution x,

$L(x)$ is the financial loss of the party harmed by pollution x.

The optimum (the efficient level of pollution) x^* is the solution to the equation

$$\Pi'(x) = L'(x).$$

If $\Pi(x)$ is a concave function and $L(x)$ is a convex function, we have a necessary and sufficient condition for efficiency.

---

94   Coase, R. H.: The Problem of Social Cost. *Journal of Law and Economics* 3, Oct. (1960): 1–44.

Figure 53: The efficient level of a negative externality

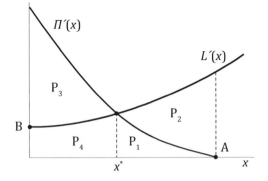

Figure 53 illustrates the polluter's decreasing marginal profit $\Pi'(x)$ and the injured party's increasing marginal loss $L'(x)$. Let's compare two possible legal regimes:

a) The law allows the polluter to damage the injured party at his will. Then, if the parties fail to agree on compensation, the outcome is the situation illustrated by point A, where the polluter ignores the loss of the injured party. At the efficient pollution level x^* (optimum compensation) the polluter will—by comparison with situation A—lose profit corresponding to area P_1 and the loss of the injured party will be reduced by the equivalent of area $P_1 + P_2$. If the parties strike a bargain and the injured party pays the polluter compensation of

$$P_1 + a \cdot P_2, \quad \text{where } 0 < a < 1,$$

to voluntarily lower its output and thereby also cut pollution, both parties will be better off at the efficient pollution level x^* relative to situation A, because
- the polluter gains $P_1 + a \cdot P_2 - P_1 = a \cdot P_2$, and
- the injured party gains $P_1 + P_2 - (P_1 + a \cdot P_2) = (1 - a) \cdot P_2$.

So, compared to situation A both parties are better off at the efficient pollution level x^*: they split the profit corresponding to area P_2.

b) The law bans pollution and the injured party can stop the polluter producing. Without compensation bargaining, the outcome is situation B, where the polluter is forced to halt production. A bargain struck between the two parties involving compensation of

$$P_4 + a \cdot P_3, \quad \text{where } 0 < a < 1$$

is again beneficial to both parties. Compared to situation B

- the polluter gains $P_3 + P_4 - (P_4 + a \cdot P_3) = (1 - a) \cdot P_3$, and
- the injured party gains $a \cdot P_3$.

So, even in legal regime b), both parties will be better off at the efficient pollution level x^* relative to situation A: they split the profit corresponding to area P_3.

Bargaining therefore leads to a Pareto-efficient solution regardless of the legal regime. However, the law does significantly influence the distribution of profit. For example, the polluter has profit (including compensation) of

- $\Pi = P_1 + a \cdot P_2 + P_3 + P_4$ when pollution is permitted, whereas
- when the injured party has the right to stop it producing, it has lower profit: $\Pi = P_3 + P_4 - (P_4 + a \cdot P_3) = (1 - a) \cdot P_3$.

In other words, from the overall perspective the legal regime is irrelevant, but from the parties' point of view it is significant.

Coasian bargaining is one of the possible ways of internalizing externalities. However, it is associated with fundamental problems. Besides the fact that bargaining costs and legal costs are not negligible in reality, there is the free rider problem. Free riders benefit from contracts to which they are not party and cannot be excluded from doing so. Another problem is the often dominant position of polluters in the emissions permit market. This can result in the polluter receiving the lion's share of the gain from bargaining.

Another internalization method is to levy on the polluter a Pigovian tax equal to the marginal damage imposed by the efficient pollution level:

$$t = \Pi'(x^*) = L'(x^*),$$

constructed in such a way as to lead the polluter to choose the efficient pollution level x^* (see Figure 54).

Figure 54: A Pigovian tax

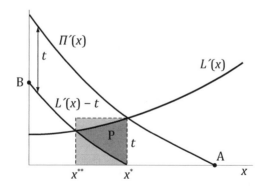

Even this approach is not free from fundamental problems. In particular, it is difficult to obtain the information necessary to calculate and determine the correct Pigovian tax. The polluter has a vested interest in distorting the information it provides to the state. There is another problem as well: if the polluter and the injured party are able to bargain, the amount of pollution will be deflected to x^{**}. This new situation is Pareto-inefficient in the sense that a shift to point x^* would increase tax revenue by $t \cdot (x^* - x^{**})$, which is more than the two agents' gain from the bargain—the dark-shaded area P in Figure 54 is necessarily a part of the rectangle with sides $t, x^* - x^{**}$.

In this sense, the combination of taxation and bargaining space is disadvantageous. The state can avoid this by using the Pigovian tax to pay the injured party a compensatory subsidy equal to the amount of damage it suffers. This will remove the injured party's incentive to negotiate compensation. The outcome is still an efficient level of pollution.[95]

The state should be interested in ensuring that environmental damage is cleaned up and environmental investment is financed by agents that can clean it up at the lowest possible cost.[96] To achieve this, however, the state does not have information about the necessary cleanup costs. What is more, there is a morally questionable principle at stake here: if the injured party (e.g. a doctor) is able to remove the problem at lower cost (e.g. by installing a noise barrier) than the originator of the negative externality (e.g. by halting confectionery production), the legal regime that permits noise pollution is surprisingly more efficient.

9.2.2 THE GENERALIZED COASE THEOREM FOR NEGATIVE EXTERNALITIES IN THE CONTEXT OF SURVIVAL PROBABILITY MAXIMIZATION

Let us now assume that both producers (the polluter and the injured party) maximize their probability of survival.

We use the following notation (with $j = 1$ denoting the polluter and $j = 2$ the injured party):

x is the amount of pollution,

$d_j(x)$ is the j-th party's income (including any compensation from the other party) at the polluter's level of activity causing pollution x,

b_j is the boundary of certain extinction of the j-th party due to low income,

---

95 This does not apply if the injured party is able to mitigate the damage caused by the polluter and the compensation varies with the amount of damage suffered. In such case the level of expenditure on mitigating the damage is lower than the efficient level. See Gravelle, H., Rees, R.: *Microeconomics*. London: Longman, pp. 516–33.

96 See Frank, R. H.: *Microeconomics and Behavior*. New York: McGraw-Hill, pp. 663–700.

$d_1(x)$ is logically an increasing function, since a greater reduction in pollution is possible only at the cost of a greater decrease in income. Conversely, $d_2(x)$ is logically decreasing, since higher pollution affects the injured party more. As it is reasonable to assume a decreasing marginal effect of a reduction in costs on the maintenance of pollution below level x, we can also assume that $d_1(x)$ is strictly concave.

We distinguish two variants for the legal regime:

A. The injured party cannot stop the polluter producing

In this variant, the injured party must pay the polluter compensation if it wants it to cut production. The final decision is up to the polluter. We use the following notation:

τ is the compensation paid by the injured party,

$x_1(\tau)$ is the injured party's variant offer, i.e. the polluter's output level at which the injured party is willing to pay it compensation τ,

$x_2(\tau)$ is the injured party's output level at the pollution level caused by the polluter's output level $x_1(\tau)$,

p_1 is the price of the polluter's output,

p_2 is the price of the injured party's output,

$\varphi_1(\tau)$ is the polluter's income (including compensation from the injured party) in relation to the amount of compensation τ.

It is reasonable to assume that $x_1(\tau)$ is a decreasing function, because a larger (smaller) reduction in output is accompanied by higher (lower) compensation. As the utility of the injured party is assumed to be the Pareto probability of survival, the level of output and the amount of compensation are bound by the condition

$$\frac{b_2}{p_2 \cdot x_2(\tau) - \tau} = \frac{b_2}{p_2 \cdot x_2^0},$$

where $x_2^0 = x_2(0)$. This implies

$$x_2(\tau) = \frac{p_2 \cdot x_2^0 + \tau}{p_2} = x_2^0 + \frac{\tau}{p_2}.$$

$$\varphi_1(\tau) = p_1 \cdot x_1(\tau) + \tau = p_1 \cdot x_1(\tau) + p_2 \cdot \left(x_2(\tau) - x_2^0 \right). \tag{*}$$

The polluter's probability of survival when the polluter is not restricted by law, pays no regard to its effect on the injured party, and is offered no compensation $(\tau = 0)$, is

$$p_1(0)=1-\frac{b_1}{\varphi_1(0)}=1-\frac{b_1}{p_1 \cdot x_1^0},$$

where $x_1^0 = x_1(0)$. The polluter's probability of survival if it accepts a subsidy of $\tau > 0$ is

$$p_1(\tau)=1-\frac{b_1}{\varphi_1(\tau)},$$

where the denominator is given by the relation (*).

The optimal amount of compensation (from the polluter's point of view) $\tau^* > 0$ must satisfy the condition $p_1'(\tau)=0$, i.e.

$$\frac{b_1 \cdot \varphi_1'(\tau^*)}{\left[\varphi_1(\tau^*)\right]^2}=0,$$

$$\varphi_1'(\tau^*)=0.$$

Substituting from relation (*):

$$\varphi_1'(\tau^*)=p_1 \cdot x_1'(\tau^*)+p_2 \cdot x_2'(\tau^*)=0.$$

So, if equation (*) has a solution $\tau^* > 0$, the maximum sum of the output of the two parties at this optimum is $p_1 \cdot x_1(\tau)+p_2 \cdot x_2(\tau)$. We can regard the following as the overall ("social") criterion, since (except for the constant $-b_1 - b_2$) it is the sum of revenues multiplied by the probability of survival for the relevant party:

$$C(\tau)=\left(1-\frac{b_1}{p_1 \cdot x_1(\tau)}\right)\cdot p_1 \cdot x_1(\tau)+\left(1-\frac{b_2}{p_2 \cdot x_2(\tau)}\right)\cdot p_2 \cdot x_2(\tau)=$$

$$=p_1 \cdot x_1(\tau)+p_2 \cdot x_2(\tau)-b_1 - b_2.$$

So, in variant A, where the polluter decides the amount of compensation based on an accommodating offer made by the injured party, these compensation negotiations produce the overall ("social") optimum.

In variant A, an environmental investment costing I and having a given environmental effect which is socially considered worth implementing (for example, through voting in a referendum), is of course financed by the injured party, whose probability of survival is thereby reduced from $\dfrac{b_2}{p_2 \cdot x_2(\tau)}$ to $\dfrac{b_2}{p_2 \cdot x_2(\tau) - I}$.

B. The injured party can stop the polluter producing

In this variant, the polluter (the party with index $j = 1$) must pay the injured party (the party with index $j = 2$) compensation for its loss. The final decision is up to the injured party and the polluter makes the variant offer. So, the injured party decides the amount of compensation and thus also the level of pollution based on the polluter's accommodating offer. We use the following notation:

 σ is the compensation paid by the polluter,

 $x_1(\sigma)$ is the polluter's variant offer, i.e. the permitted output level requested by the polluter in return for compensation σ,

 $x_2(\tau)$ is the injured party's output level at the pollution level caused by the polluter's output level $x_1(\tau)$,

 p_1 is the price of the polluter's output,

 p_2 is the price of the injured party's output,

 $\varphi_1(\sigma)$ is the polluter's income (net of compensation paid to the injured party) in relation to the amount of compensation σ.

Here we assume that the variant offer $x_1(\sigma)$ is an increasing function, because higher compensation means a higher permitted level of pollution. Maximization of the probability of survival by the polluter leads to the condition

$$\frac{b_1}{p_1 \cdot x_1(\sigma) - \sigma} = \frac{b_1}{p_1 \cdot x_1^0},$$

where $x_1^0 = x_1(0)$. For the polluter's offer this implies

$$x_1(\sigma) = \frac{p_1 \cdot x_1^0 + \sigma}{p_1} = x_1^0 + \frac{\sigma}{p_1},$$

$$\varphi_2(\sigma) = p_2 \cdot x_2(\sigma) + \sigma = p_2 \cdot x_2(\tau) + p_1 \cdot \left(x_1(\tau) - x_1^0\right). \tag{**}$$

The injured party's probability of survival if it accepts no compensation ($\sigma = 0$) is

$$p_2(0)=1-\frac{b_2}{\varphi_2(0)}=1-\frac{b_2}{p_2\cdot x_2^0},$$

where $x_2^0 = x_2(0)$. The injured party's probability of survival if it accepts a subsidy of $\sigma > 0$ is

$$p_2(\sigma)=1-\frac{b_2}{\varphi_2(\sigma)},$$

where the denominator is given by relation (**).

The optimal amount of compensation (from the polluter's point of view) $\sigma^* > 0$ must satisfy the condition $p_2'(\sigma)=0$. After substituting in the same way as in variant A we get

$$\varphi_2'(\sigma^*)=0.$$

Substituting from relation (**):

$$\varphi_2'(\sigma^*)=p_1\cdot x_1'(\sigma^*)+p_2\cdot x_2'(\sigma^*)=0.$$

If an optimum exists (i.e. equation (**) has a solution $\sigma^* > 0$), the value of the "social" criterion $C(\sigma)$ here, as in variant A, is at a maximum.

For both variant A and variant B, the decision-taker's optimum is identical to the overall ("social") optimum.

The same cannot be said, however, for environmental investment. In the standard Coase theorem it does not matter "socially" what the legal regime is (and who, therefore, finances this investment), but in generalized microeconomics it does matter.

The value of the "social" criterion after the implementation of investment I in variant A is

$$C^{(A)}(\tau)=\left(1-\frac{b_1}{p_1\cdot x_1(\tau^*)}\right)\cdot p_1\cdot x_1(\tau)+\left(1-\frac{b_2}{p_2\cdot x_2(\tau)-I}\right)\cdot p_2\cdot x_2(\tau),$$

whereas the value of the criterion after the implementation of investment I in variant B is

$$C^{(B)}(\tau)=\left(1-\frac{b_1}{p_1\cdot x_1(\tau^*)-I}\right)\cdot p_1\cdot x_1(\tau)+\left(1-\frac{b_2}{p_2\cdot x_2(\tau)}\right)\cdot p_2\cdot x_2(\tau),$$

where the following certainly applies (except in the totally unrealistic and exceptional case $b_1 = b_2$ & $p_1 \cdot x_1(\tau^*) = p_2 \cdot x_2(\tau^*)$):

$$C^{(A)}(\tau) \neq C^{(B)}(\tau).$$

On the basis of these conclusions we can now formulate the following theorem:

Generalized Coase theorem for negative externalities
From the point of view of generalized economics, where agents maximize their own Pareto probability of survival, it holds that:

- allowing two parties to negotiate compensation for environmental damage will lead to optimization of the utility of both parties and of social utility regardless of the legal regime. In this respect, there is no difference from the Coase theorem in standard microeconomics with the *homo economicus* paradigm. By contrast,
- in generalized economics (as distinct from the Coase theorem in standard microeconomics) the legal regime will influence the individual and social "costs" (compared in the criteria of individuals and of society as a whole under consideration) of investment in environmental cleanup. If the legal regime disadvantages the party that is more threatened, these "costs" are higher than in the opposite case.

9.2.3 THE COASE THEOREM FOR THE CASE WHERE A PRODUCER HARMS A CONSUMER

In this case it makes sense to consider the restrictive regime only, with consumers being willing to allow the producer to pollute in return for certain compensation. We will assume that there is an authority—for example the state—that defends the interests of all injured parties simultaneously. How much does this change the conclusions derived above?

The difference here is that consumers do not have a profit criterion. Their decision-making can of course be modelled using a function representing the amount that consumers would regard as sufficient compensation for their losses. In that case we can proceed in the same way as in the previous section. The problem, however, lies in establishing the shape of this compensation function.

We do not consider sociological surveys to be very useful for solving this problem. Answers to questions such as "What proportion of your income are you willing to forgo in compensation for a reduction in the pollution level by one ton per square mile?" are always hypothetical. The payment is not real and the assessment is very subjective and can differ significantly from person to person in terms of the amount and of the credibility of the figure. It is hard to imagine constructing a reliable compensation function in such a way.

One possible way of establishing the shape of the compensation function is provided by the Tiebout model. It assumes that individuals will (if allowed to) form communities with similar preferences.[97] People "vote with their feet". Those who prefer higher taxes and lower pollution will move to "green havens". These havens, however, will be unaffordable for the poor, who, conversely, will move to high-pollution locations. This will clearly not be the overall (globally) optimal solution. The benefit of this model, however, is that it reveals preferences, which can be used to help us establish the shape of the compensation function.

We can, however, view the problem symmetrically as an effort to achieve the maximum utility from a positive externality. This allows us to use the methodology set out in the next section.

9.3 THE COASE THEOREM FOR POSITIVE EXTERNALITIES

The fundamental principle of the Coase theorem applies to positive externalities as well as to negative ones. If the output chosen by an externality provider when maximizing its own income is low from the perspective of the recipient of the externality, the recipient can financially stimulate the provider. In this case we focus on the survival probability maximization model.

The Coase theorem states that maximization of the private utility of the parties will generate the "socially" optimal outcome. Any external directive or regulation will inevitably spoil this outcome.

The application of the Coase theorem to positive externalities has some specific features. It involves redistribution rather than compensation for damage caused to another party—one agent provides support to another in whose survival and increased activity it has an economic interest. Rather than altruism (which we will discuss in the final chapter of this book), it is therefore a case of action motivated by the donor's own economic benefit.

9.3.1 THE GENERALIZED COASE THEOREM FOR POSITIVE EXTERNALITIES AND AGENTS MAXIMIZING THEIR OWN SURVIVAL PROBABILITY

We take as our example the relationship between an apple grower (orchard owner) and a beekeeper. There are two possibilities: either we can assume that the number of beehives is insufficient to ensure cross-pollination of the apple

---

97   See Tiebout, C.: The Pure Theory of Local Expenditure. *Journal of Political Economy* 64, 5(1956): 416–24.

grower's trees and so the apple grower is willing, in his own interest, to subsidize the beekeeper; or, conversely, we can assume that the number of trees is too low to provide enough pollen for the hives and so the beekeeper—also in his own interest—will donate funds to the apple grower so that he can expand his orchard.

Suppose, for example, that the bees are the "bottleneck", i.e. that the orchard owner is the recipient of the positive externality. From the purely modelling perspective, the opposite case merely involves renumbering the parties.

Furthermore, let us assume that the survival of both parties, namely the provider and the recipient of the positive externality, depends exclusively on their income.

The sales revenue e_s of the recipient of the positive externality (the apple grower) comes exclusively from the sale of apples of quantity q_s at unit price π_s, i.e. the sales revenue of the apple grower is $e_s = q_s \cdot \pi_s$. Let us assume for simplicity that $q_s = 0$ if the provider of the positive externality (the beekeeper) goes out of business. The income of the apple grower, which provides the beekeeper with a subsidy of σ, is $d_s = e_s - \sigma$.

The income d_v of the provider of the positive externality (the beekeeper) comes partly from the sale of honey of quantity q_v at unit price π_v, and partly from the subsidy provided by the orchard owner σ, i.e. $d_v = e_v + \sigma$, where $e_v = q_v \cdot \pi_v$.

Let us assume that in both cases these are the agents' sole sources of income. In line with the other chapters of this book, we assume that the risk of extinction of an agent with income d and subsistence level b is determined by his relative margin vis-à-vis the subsistence level $\dfrac{d-b}{d} = 1 - \dfrac{b}{d}$, which is consistent with a first-order Pareto distribution.[98] Let us denote the subsistence level b (the extinction zone boundary) of the orchard owner (the recipient of the positive externality) by b_0 and that of the beekeeper (the provider of the positive externality) by b_1.

9.3.2 SINGLE POSITIVE EXTERNALITY PROVIDER MODEL

Let us assume that the apple grower's output q_s is a smooth increasing function of honey output q_v:

$$q_s = q_s (q_v).$$

---

98 See Chapter 1.

The apple price π_s (like the honey price π_v) is given, so the apple grower's sales revenue function is also a smooth increasing function:

$$e_s(q_v) = \pi_s \cdot q_s(q_v).$$

Let us furthermore assume that the beekeeper's output q_v is also given and that there is a risk that the beekeeper will go out of business (owing to insufficient income) and his output will fall to zero. His income is

$$d_v = e_v + \sigma = q_v \cdot \pi_v + \sigma$$

and his survival probability is

$$p_v(\sigma) = \frac{d_v - b_v}{d_v} = 1 - \frac{b_v}{q_v \cdot \pi_v + \sigma}.$$

By contrast, the apple grower is in a situation of two threats: first due to low income of his own, and second due to the beekeeper going out of business. The apple grower's income for his own needs (net of the subsidy he provides to the beekeeper) is

$$d_s = \pi_s \cdot e_s(q_v) - \sigma$$

and his probability of survival is given by the product of the probability of survival of the beekeeper and the probability of the apple grower avoiding extinction due to low own income:

$$p_s(\sigma) = \left[1 - \frac{b_v}{q_v \cdot \pi_v + \sigma} \right] \cdot \left[1 - \frac{b_s}{\pi_s \cdot q_s(q_v) - \sigma} \right].$$

Let us denote the first factor by C_1 and the second one by C_0:

$$p_0(\sigma) = C_1(\sigma) \cdot C_0(\sigma).$$

The condition for a maximum is

$$C_1'(\sigma) \cdot C_0(\sigma) + C_0'(\sigma) \cdot C_1(\sigma) = 0,$$

$$\frac{C_1'(\sigma)}{C_1(\sigma)} = -\frac{C_0'(\sigma)}{C_0(\sigma)},$$

$$[\ln C_1(\sigma)]' = -[\ln C_0(\sigma)]'.$$

Because the derived functions on either side of the equation are (given the assumed smoothness of function $q_s(q_v)$) simple, strictly monotonic, smooth and positive, and because $[\ln C_1(0)]' < -[\ln C_0(0)]'$ and $\lim_{\sigma \to \infty}[\ln C_1(\sigma)]' > -\lim_{\sigma \to \infty}[\ln C_0(\sigma)]'$, there exists a single optimum subsidy level σ^*. It is clear that for this level $\sigma^* > 0$, i.e. if there is a single beekeeper in the locality it is economically advantageous for the orchard owner to subsidize him regardless of the parameters of the model.

9.3.3 MULTIPLE POSITIVE EXTERNALITY PROVIDERS MODEL

We will start by analysing the situation with two beekeepers. Will the apple grower choose one of them, or will it support both? Will it prefer the stronger one (providing him with a greater degree of security than the weaker one) or the weaker one (the existence of two beekeepers may suit the apple grower more)? Will the fact that there are two beekeepers affect the amount of the subsidy? Our approach, as we will demonstrate, allows us to analyse such non-trivial problems.

We assume that the apple grower will go out of business only if both beekeepers do likewise. His survival probability is therefore given by the relation:

$$P_s(\sigma_1,\sigma_2) = \left[1 - \frac{b_s}{\pi_s \cdot q_s(q_v) - \sigma}\right] \cdot \left[1 - \frac{b_v^1}{q_v^1 \cdot \pi_v + \sigma_1}\right] \cdot \left[1 - \frac{b_v^2}{q_v^2 \cdot \pi_v + \sigma - \sigma_1}\right]$$

and honey output will be divided (at the same overall volume) into the output of the two beekeepers: $q_v = q_v^1 + q_v^2$.

Let us start by assuming that the two beekeepers are in an equal economic position, i.e. $b_v^1 = b_v^2$, $q_v^1 = q_v^2 = q_v/2$ and are therefore equally at risk of extinction. In this case, of course, the apple grower has no reason to prefer one beekeeper over the other (from his perspective they are identical), so we can assume that $\sigma_1 = \sigma_2 = \sigma/2$. The apple grower's probability of survival is then:

$$P_s\left(\frac{\sigma}{2},\frac{\sigma}{2}\right) = \left[1 - \frac{b_s}{\pi_s \cdot q_s(e_v) - \sigma}\right] \cdot \left[1 - \frac{2b_v}{q_v \cdot \pi_v + \sigma}\right]^2.$$

If the beekeepers are in an unequal economic position, the apple grower will prefer the weaker one. If the probability of extinction of the weaker one will remain higher even after receiving the entire subsidy σ, it will get the entire subsidy. If not, the subsidy will be split as follows:

$$\sigma_1 = \sigma_0 + (\sigma - \sigma_0)/2,$$

$$\sigma_2 = (\sigma - \sigma_0)/2,$$

where σ_0 is the subsidy that balances the threats to both, i.e.

$$1 - \frac{b_v^{\;1}}{d_v^{\;1} + \sigma_0} = 1 - \frac{b_v^{\;2}}{d_v^{\;2}}.$$

For n beekeepers having the same economic position, the subsidy will be split equally, i.e. $\sigma_j = \sigma/n$, and the following will hold for the apple grower's probability of survival, similarly as in the $n = 2$ case:

$$P_s\left(\frac{\sigma}{n}, ..., \frac{\sigma}{n}\right) = \left[1 - \frac{b_s}{\pi_s \cdot q_s(e_v) - \sigma}\right] \cdot \left[1 - \frac{n \cdot b_v}{q_v \cdot \pi_v + \sigma}\right]^n.$$

By providing the same overall subsidy σ to multiple beekeepers, the apple grower will increase his probability of survival. The higher the number of beekeepers n, the lower the increase in his survival probability. We have proved this by conducting computer experiments for the case where there are two beekeepers in an equal economic position and the orchard owner's sales revenues are 10 times as high as the beekeepers' combined sales revenues. The results of these experiments are shown in Figure 55.

Figure 55: The increase in the apple grower's probability of survival (on the vertical axis) as a result of his subsidy to n beekeepers in % of own income (on the horizontal axis)

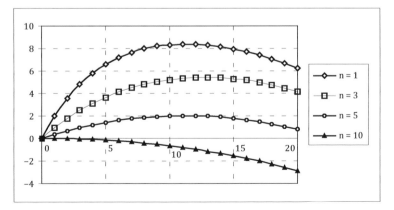

The effect of the subsidy (of around 10% of the apple grower's income overall at the optimum point) is therefore the highest for the single beekeeper case.

This conclusion is logical: the smaller the number of beekeepers, the larger the risk posed to the apple grower by a threat to any one of them, and hence *ceteris paribus* the greater the incentive to provide a subsidy. With a higher number of beekeepers, the apple grower will reduce the subsidy (because by providing the subsidy he is causing a threat to himself by reducing his income). If the number of agents providing the positive externality is very high, the orchard owner will stop providing the subsidy.

These conclusions are obviously conditional on the highly restrictive and simplifying assumptions of the model. Nevertheless, we can derive from them some rules that apply in reality. The same is true for a model constructed for a specific positive externality, namely for information.

9.4 EFFICIENCY OF ACQUISITION AND TRANSFER OF INFORMATION BETWEEN AGENTS THAT DEPEND ON EACH OTHER TO SURVIVE

In this section we examine the efficiency of acquisition and transfer of information between two private agents where one agent provides a vital positive externality of a tangible nature to the other.

Information (e.g. technical knowledge) can be a public good (e.g. a mathematical formula) or a purely private good (e.g. the recipe for a herbal liqueur). Some information and technology is generally usable (e.g. a weather forecast), while other knowledge may be tied to a particular product (e.g. a computer program). Both information and an intermediary service reducing a perceived lack of information can meanwhile be a private good: in this case the economic agent (decision-taker) compares the price or marginal cost with the marginal benefit and then decides whether or not to buy the information. This is a standard market mechanism involving supply and demand for an economic good— in this case information.

However, information can also be provided as a gift, i.e. free of charge, if it has the character of a positive externality where the decision-taker's economic outcome (or even economic survival) is tied to the existence of another agent. The recipient of the positive externality may then have an interest, for example, in increasing the technological level of this agent and acquiring and transferring technological information to it, perhaps even free of charge, but nonetheless in its own interest. This form of support can be better for the provider than a direct subsidy, for which there is a risk of fungibility (i.e. use for a different purpose than for the externality in question).[99]

99　We address this problem in more detail in the final chapter of this book, on the economically rational provision of subsidies. We also give references to relevant literature there.

A willingness to fund the acquisition and transfer of information justi-fied by such a positive externality is (alongside trading in intangible assets, of course) one of the possible microeconomic incentives for technology diffusion in an economic system.[100] In the following section we show that the generalized microeconomics approach can be useful for describing this process.

Let us assume that the survival of two agents, namely the provider and the recipient of information as a positive externality, depends exclusively on their income. Moreover, the survival of the provider of information is conditional on the survival of the recipient of that information, which is providing it with a vi-tal positive externality. The fate of the recipient of this externality is therefore tied to that of the recipient of the information. Consequently, if the information recipient goes out of business, so will the information provider.

We assume that the sales revenue (income) e_0 of the information provider comes exclusively from the sale of quantity x_0 of its product at unit price p_0, i.e.

$$e_0 = x_0 \cdot p_0.$$

The provider's income is

$$d_0 = e_0 - \mu,$$

where μ is the cost of acquiring and transferring the information.

9.4.1 MODEL A: INFORMATION EFFECT = INFORMATION ACQUISITION AND TRANSFER COST

Let us start by assuming an extreme situation where the cost of acquiring the information equals the benefit of the information to the recipient thereof.

We again assume that the risk of extinction of an agent with income d and subsistence level b is determined by his relative margin vis-à-vis the subsist-ence level

$$r(d,b) = \frac{d-b}{d} = 1 - \frac{b}{d},$$

which is consistent with a first-order Pareto probability distribution as de-scribed in section 1.3.1.

We will denote the subsistence levels (extinction zone boundaries) of the two agents by b_0 and b_1.

---

100 For more on technology diffusion, see Hlaváček, M.: Modely difuze technologií. *WP IES* No. 1, Praha: Fakulta sociálních věd UK, 2001.

The information recipient (threatened exclusively by low income) has income of

$$d_1 = e_1 + \mu,$$

which corresponds to a survival probability of

$$p_1(\mu) = 1 - \frac{b_1}{d_1} = 1 - \frac{b_1}{e_1 + \mu}.$$

By contrast, the information provider is in a situation of two threats: first due to low income of his own, and second due to the information recipient going out of business. The information provider's income is

$$d_0 = e_0 - \mu,$$

which corresponds to a survival probability given by the product of the probability of survival of the information recipient and the probability of the information provider avoiding extinction due to low own income:

$$p_0(\mu) = \left[1 - \frac{b_1}{e_1 + \mu} \right] \cdot \left[1 - \frac{b_0}{e_0 - \mu} \right].$$

Let us assume that the two agents are—prior to the decision to acquire and transfer information—in the position of the median of the relevant set (in terms of income level), which, for the assumed Pareto distribution of income, is double the survival zone boundary level:

$$e_0 = 2 \cdot b_0,$$

$$e_1 = 2 \cdot b_1.$$

Let us denote the ratio of the sizes of the two agents, measured by their income, by k:

$$e_0 = k \cdot e_1,$$

$$b_0 = k \cdot b_1,$$

i.e. we assume that the provider's income and its extinction zone boundary are k times the corresponding variable for the information recipient.

We choose the money unit in such a way that $b_1 = 1$. Under this assumption:

$b_0 = k \cdot e_1 = 2,$

$e_0 = 2 \cdot k,$

$b_0 = k.$

The information provider's survival probability here is:

$$p(\mu,k) = \left[1 - \frac{1}{2+\mu}\right] \cdot \left[1 - \frac{k}{2k-\mu}\right] = \frac{1+\mu}{2+\mu} \cdot \frac{k-\mu}{2k-\mu}.$$

Let us set k as the parameter of the maximization problem. Differentiating $p(\mu,k)$ with respect to μ and setting this derivative equal to zero gives us the condition for a maximum in the form of an equation with unknown μ and parameter k:

$$(k - 1 - 2\mu) \cdot (2 + \mu) \cdot (2k - \mu) - (2k - 2 - 2\mu) \cdot (1 + \mu) \cdot (k - \mu) = 0.$$

In Figure 56 the root of this equation is shown on the vertical axis as a function of parameter k on the horizontal axis:

Figure 56: Information provision and transfer cost μ versus parameter k (the ratio of the information provider's income to the information recipient's income)—model A

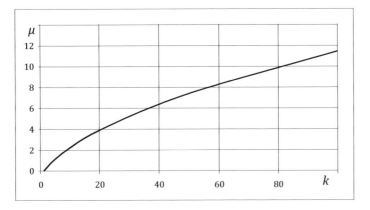

It is also interesting to look at the relationship between the share of support in the donor's income μ/d and the ratio of the sizes of the two agents k:

Figure 57: The optimal share of support in the donor's income μ/d versus the ratio of the sizes of the information provider and the information recipient—model A

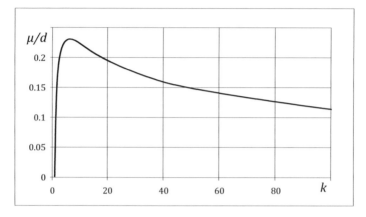

It turns out that an agent with 6.5 times the income of the information recipient will donate the maximum proportion of its income for the acquisition and transfer of information. If the two agents are equal in size (i.e. if $k = 1$), the optimal level of support is zero. For increasing k the optimal proportion decreases, and for $k \to \infty$ it also tends to zero. However, for $k = 1000$ it is still greater than 4%.

We will now conduct an analysis of sensitivity to the size of the information effect. *Ceteris paribus* we will change the model by making the effect of the transferred information half as large as the information acquisition cost.

9.4.2 MODEL B: INFORMATION EFFECT < INFORMATION ACQUISITION AND TRANSFER COST

The information recipient (threatened exclusively by low income) now has income of

$$d_1 = e_1 + \frac{\mu}{2}$$

and a survival probability of

$$p_1(\sigma) = 1 - \frac{b_1}{d_1} = 1 - \frac{b_1}{e_1 + \dfrac{\mu}{2}}.$$

The information provider is again in a situation of two threats: first due to low income of his own, and second due to the information recipient going out of business. As in model A, his income is

$$d_0 = e_0 - \mu.$$

The information provider's survival probability is again given by the product of the probability of survival of the information recipient and the probability of the information provider avoiding extinction due to low own income:

$$p_0(\sigma) = \left[1 - \frac{b_1}{e_1 + \dfrac{\mu}{2}} \right] \cdot \left[1 - \frac{b_0}{e_0 - \mu} \right].$$

We again assume that the two agents are (prior to the decision to acquire and transfer information) in the position of the median of the relevant set (in terms of income level), which, for the Pareto income distribution, is double the survival zone boundary level. We also choose the money unit in the same way as in model A. The information provider's maximized survival probability is then:

$$p(\mu,k) = \left[1 - \frac{b_1}{2 + \dfrac{\mu}{2}} \right] \cdot \left[1 - \frac{k}{2k - \mu} \right] = \frac{2 + \mu}{4 + \mu} \cdot \frac{k - \mu}{2k - \mu}.$$

Differentiating $p(\mu, k)$ with respect to μ and setting this derivative equal to zero again gives us the condition for a maximum, this time in the form:

$$(k - 2 - 2\mu) \cdot (4 + \mu) \cdot (2k - \mu) - (2k - 4 - 2\mu) \cdot (2 + \mu) \cdot (k - \mu) = 0.$$

Figures 58 and 59 show how the optimal support varies in absolute terms and in relative terms (in relation to income) as a function of parameter k, i.e. the ratio of the sizes of the two agents:

It is noteworthy that even in model B, where the effect of the information is lower than the cost of acquiring and transferring it, the acquisition and transfer of information is advantageous for both agents (advantageousness being assessed here on the basis of the agents' probability of survival).

There is another, even more surprising finding: it is not true that the greater is the information effect, the stronger is the incentive for both agents. Above a certain threshold[101], an increase in the disproportion in the two agents' sizes

---

101 The threshold value of the parameter in our illustrative example was $k = 8$. For a different choice of model parameters the threshold is different.

increases the proportion of support provided from the income of the support provider.

Figure 58: The absolute size of the provider's support for information acquisition and transfer versus parameter _k_ (ratio of the sizes of the information provider and the information recipient)—model B

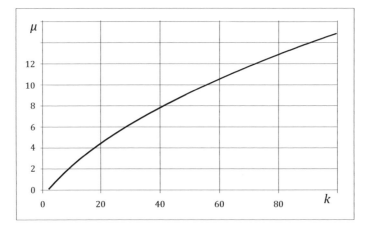

Figure 59: The share of support for information acquisition and transfer in the provider's income versus parameter _k_ (ratio of the sizes of the information provider and the information recipient)—model B

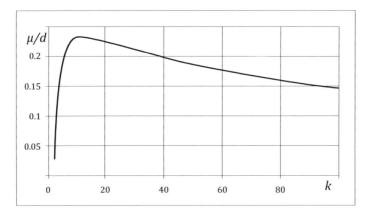

Figure 60: Comparison of the share of support in the income of the support provider for model A (solid line) and model B (dashed line)

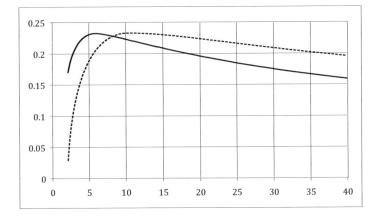

10.

ALTRUISM AND REDISTRIBUTION
INCREASING THE PROBABILITY
OF SURVIVAL OF INDIVIDUALS

10.1 ALTRUISM AND BELONGING TO THE COMMUNITY

Standard microeconomics deals with selfish individuals who are interested solely in their own welfare. However, interest in the welfare of others also figures in the economic behaviour of most individuals. Every individual is—to some extent—willing to give up his own benefit (e.g. money) for the benefit of his fellow man. This is an expression of belonging to the community,[102] where the individual is (or feels to be) a member of this community, for example belonging to family, firm, town or country or just the community of decent people.

Altruism and belonging to the community are a natural part of human ethics. The classical economist Adam Smith was astonished by the human emphasis on the ethical aspect of human behaviour, which, even on the economic level, is not determined solely by personal prosperity.[103]

---

102 This issued is studied in Hlaváček, J. et al.: *Mikroekonomie sounáležitosti se společenstvím*. Praha: Karolinum, 1999.

103 "How selfish soever man may be supposed, there are evidently some principles in his nature, which interest him in the fortune of others, and render their happiness necessary to him, though he derives nothing from it, except the pleasure of seeing it." See Smith, A.: *The Theory of Moral Sentiments*. New Rochelle, NY: Arlington House, 1969 (first published in 1759). In his theory of altruism, Adam Smith described a relationship of strong practical incentives and weak ethical incentives (principles) as the mechanism of suppression of self-interest.

Altruistic behaviour can be explained in evolutionary terms:[104] a higher degree of solidarity among the members of a community, as evidenced, for example, by a greater degree of redistribution, usually[105] *ceteris paribus* increases that community's odds of survival in the struggle for survival against other groups.

Altruism, and even "hard-core" altruism[106], can therefore be understood in terms of our generalized economics if we treat it as a special case of belonging to the community.[107] If an individual feels mutuality with other individuals and regards them as part of himself ("me"), the provision of financial support at the expense of purely personal gain is a decision that can be explained by maximization of his personal probability of survival. A community member displays aversion not only to situations with a high economic threat to his own person, but also to situations with a high economic threat to other community members.

Altruism and belonging to the community are not a consequence of exclusively rational thinking, of course. Yet even here, there are economically rational and irrational decisions, for instance when a donor distributes a subsidy among multiple recipients.

Altruism may lie outside the mainstream of standard microeconomics, but it is by no means a neglected issue. Many economists—from the aforementioned Adam Smith through to Nobel prize winners Herbert Simon and Gary Becker—have described and analysed the causes of altruistic behaviour.[108]

---

104 See Axelrod, G.: *The Evolution of Cooperation.* New York: Basic Books, 1981.

105 Not necessarily. In certain cases an altruist can threaten a community by irrational self-sacrifice. For instance, an extreme sacrifice by one member of a family can jeopardize his personal survival and thereby destroy the family. For more details, see Hlaváček, J. et al.: *Mikroekonomie sounáležitosti se společenstvím.* Praha: Karolinum, 1999, pp. 151–55.

106 Altruism motivated by expected compensation is referred to as "soft-core" altruism. If a donor expects no compensation, we speak of "hard-core" altruism. The distinction between hard-core and soft-core altruism was introduced by the founder of sociobiology E. O. Wilson. See Wilson, E. O.: *On Human Nature.* Cambridge: Harvard University Press, 1978.

107 See Etzioni, A.: The Moral Dimension. Toward a New Economics. New York: The Free Press, 1988. The way Etzioni sees it, "I" contains "we", which is a part of every individual. According to Etzioni, the social and moral dimension of human preferences enhances the stability and usually also the quality of economic decision-making.

108 See, for example, Simon, H. A.: A Mechanism for Social Selection and Successful Altruism. *Science* 250, 4488(1990): 1665–68, and also Becker, G. S.: The Theory of Social Interactions. *Journal of Political Economy* 82, 6(1974): 1063–93 or Becker, G. S.: Altruism, Egoism and Genetic Fitness: Economics and Sociobiology. *Journal of Economic Literature* 14, 3(1976): 817–26. In Czech, see, for example, Klusoň, V.: *Instituce a odpovědnost: K filosofii ekonomické vědy.* Praha: Karolinum, 2004, or Mlčoch, L.: *Ekonomie důvěry a společného dobra.* Praha: Karolinum, 2006.

10.2 REDISTRIBUTION

Extensive redistribution (reallocation of the results of productive activity in some other way than purely on the market for factors of production) is a part of every economy in the modern world. It has also been a part of human history since time immemorial. Recipients of income from productive activity provide a proportion of that income to needy fellow citizens and/or the poor in other parts of the world in the form of alms, gifts, sponsorship or charity donations. Taxes—vital for funding state pension and social security systems and for financing public goods—are another form of redistribution.

Neoclassical microeconomics, however, more or less ignores this phenomenon. It argues that in conditions of microeconomic equilibrium, the distribution of the results of economic activity in a market economy corresponds to the gains (marginal product) of the individual agents involved. If an agent's economic activity is to be maximally efficient, the distribution of the results must correspond to the marginal product of the individual factors of production and of the individual agents. Hence, a profit-maximizing model firm will pay an employee a wage equal to the marginal product of that employee's labour, the rent on agricultural land will correspond to the marginal product of that land, and so on. The profit of an entrepreneur (assuming free market entry) will be at a standard level that can be derived from the marginal product of capital.

This distribution is consistent with market logic (especially given perfect competition), so redistribution is treated by microeconomics de facto as a violation of efficiency resulting from the fact that the economy does not consist solely of agents matching the *homo economicus* paradigm. In standard microeconomics, economic (i.e. profit-seeking, exclusively own-material-gain maximizing) behaviour in the narrower sense is the norm, while redistribution is in some way imperfect and flawed.

Yet it is precisely at this point that economics, with its "economic man" paradigm (*homo economicus* agents maximizing their own prosperity subject to given constraints), departs from reality. The Darwinian principle of survival of the fittest (which to a large extent also holds for economic institutions and relations) has led advanced societies to redistribute approximately 50 per cent of the income they generate. Over the last 100 years the redistribution-to-income ratio of advanced economies has been rising, and the living standards of redistribution-dependent households have been rising even faster. This leads us to believe that it is wrong to dismiss redistribution as a "flaw in the system" or a "non-economic phenomenon" and that, on the contrary, the taking into account of the joys and sorrows of others is a highly economic phenomenon. The incidence of altruistic and cooperative traits in individuals' economic preferences and the fact that social cohesion can be classed among the determinants of growth and among the necessary conditions for sustainable economic development are consistent with this belief.

To construct descriptive models of redistribution in various decision-taking situations, we need to understand the motivation of the individuals involved and identify the reasons why people often take into account the joys and sorrows of others, be it directly by supporting those close to them or indirectly by accepting taxation, where the state intermediates the redistribution process.

10.2.1 THE SUPPLY SIDE OF REDISTRIBUTION (THE WILLINGNESS TO FORGO PART OF ONE'S PERSONAL PROSPERITY) DERIVED FROM THE SOCIAL NATURE OF INDIVIDUALS' PREFERENCES

As mentioned earlier, human individuals group together and form communities in the interests of their own survival. A necessary condition for establishing and maintaining a community is mutual trust. Greater mutual trust implies an economically stronger and longer-lasting community. This holds not only for communities such as firms, but also for economies as a whole.[109]

Appropriate control and regulatory authorities of higher instance, in particular the state, can enhance mutual trust and, as a result, strengthen the economy as a whole. Such control and regulation constitutes *sui generis* a positive externality. It reduces—at the state's expense—how much individuals need to spend on determining whether a potential business partner is reliable, on hiring legal services, on creating reserves against unpredictable action by uncooperative business partners, and so on.

Our approach to modelling these problems involves generalization of the agent's economic criterion as applied in this book, in the sense that we assume that the agent is averse to situations that entail a high probability of extinction, including extinction of other agents or of the community. Minimization of the probability of extinction enables us to compare different extinction threats. The case of a single threat—that of a lack of money—accords with the standard rationality of *homo economicus.*

There are many reasons for taking into account the joys and sorrows of others. In the following sections we will describe at least the most important of them in detail.

---

109 Fukuyama, R.: *Trust: The Social Virtues and the Creation of Prosperity.* London: Hamish Hamilton 1995, proved empirically that economically advanced states display a higher degree of trust (by comparison with other states) in relations between economic agents, primarily as a result of high transaction costs in poorer economies with a lower degree of trust.

10.2.1.1 TAKING INTO ACCOUNT THE INTERESTS OF OTHERS WHEN SUCH ACTION DIRECTLY INCREASES THE PROSPERITY OF THE INDIVIDUAL ("PSEUDO-ALTRUISM")

This motive explains social behaviour within the framework of the neoclassical *homo economicus* paradigm. It covers, for example:

- the forgoing of immediate profit by a firm in order to enhance its reputation and thereby increase its future profits,
- conspicuous giving by individuals in order to increase their social standing,
- sports or cultural sponsorship that a firm can use in its marketing to increase its profits,
- the funding of a political party by a firm in order to increase its chances of penetrating a lucrative restricted market (insurance, banking, pharmaceuticals, etc.) or of winning a lucrative central or local government contract,
- the finding that cooperative behaviour—enabling membership in the set of "reputable firms"—reduces the costs of checking the integrity of economic partners.[110]

All these manifestations of unselfish behaviour can be explained by standard microeconomics. They are de facto cases of rigorous application of the principles contained in the *homo economicus* paradigm.

10.2.1.2 THE UNCALCULATED NEEDED TO DO GOOD (HARD-CORE ALTRUISM)

Uncalculated selflessness is a characteristic of human behaviour. Examples include:

- the urge to protect one's own and others' children, the elderly and the frail from material hardship,
- the urge to provide alms (anonymously, without calculating, for internal reasons only),
- the sense of wrongdoing associated with refusing the outstretched hands of a beggar.

These are actions in which the altruistic urge manifests itself irrationally, "without cause" and without logical explanation, and is directed exclusively at

---

110 This is illustrated by Frank's parable of the hawks and doves. See Frank, R. H.: *Microeconomics and Behavior.* New York: McGraw-Hill, 2006, pp. 236–39.

the benefit (survival) of others. This "hard-core altruism", described in more detail in section 10.1, can lead to self-sacrifice in favour of another individual or the community

Manifestations of altruism towards unrelated human beings were and are a necessary condition for belonging to the community per se, and are therefore a consequence of biological evolution.

We believe that these reasons for unselfish behaviour cannot be explained by economics (not even generalized microeconomics) in any other way than simply as a biologically given part of an individual's motives. Such altruism does not involve deciding between alternatives—an individual either does or does not have an unselfish motive. If he does, the problem can be modelled using generalized microeconomics, for example by maximizing the probability of simultaneous survival of the decision-taker and the person or community he is protecting and analysing the impacts of this maximization on the distribution of economic goods between them. We describe such models in section 10.3.

10.2.1.3 RECIPROCAL ALTRUISM

Reciprocity can also be a motive for altruistic behaviour. An individual does good in the expectation (backed by his own experience or by experience learned, for example, from his parents or from books) that those around him will do likewise. Manifestations of responsibility (provided and expected) towards related and non-related vulnerable individuals are a necessary condition for cohesion and for the ability of human society to survive and are therefore a result of biological and cultural evolution and cannot be derived from purely economic motives.

10.2.1.4 THE URGE OF INDIVIDUALS TO GROUP TOGETHER IN CLUBS

Individuals have a specific interest in taking part in club activities. Clubs are based on mutual support among agents bound by a common interest. They arise in situations where individuals have, for example, a common hobby and where the pursuit of that hobby is conditional on having common property (e.g. a playing field or gym), as none of the individuals can afford such property on their own. The same property often provides a benefit—a positive externality (for instance the ability to attend a football match)—to non-members of the club. In such case, the running of the club is funded partly from private capital and partly from public capital.

Something similar applies in the case of the prosperity of a town, to which its citizens are the main contributors. The citizens' sense of belonging to the local community makes local taxes and voluntary work more acceptable to them.

In addition to clubs, various coalitions, lobbies and political groups are formed on the basis of mutuality. Although these often appear to be defending the public interest, what they are really trying to do is gain an advantage over the "rest of the world".

An interesting theory dealing with this issue is Buchanan's economic theory of clubs,[111] which regards a club good as a cross between a purely public good and a purely private good. Club goods are rivalrous and excludable and partly have the character of public goods, although only within a given group of consumers (the club). The group (club) is the owner of the good and shares the acquisition costs and utility arising from it. Solidarity with the club prevents the danger of overuse of the good, so there is no risk of Hayek's "tragedy of the commons".[112]

On the other hand, club goods may be exposed to the opposite danger, referred to as the "tragedy of the anticommons".[113] This danger consists in the under-use of resources as a result of the over-restriction of consumption. Here, by contrast, solidarity with the club can exacerbate the problem if very limited and exclusive membership is seen as shared utility and so the existing members block an otherwise economically rational reduction in the annual club membership fee through the taking on of new members. Such membership in an exclusive and expensive club represents a switch from conspicuous leisure (characterizing the leisure class) to conspicuous consumption.[114]

Generalized microeconomics gives us some ability to model the relationship between the individual and the club. Suppose, for example, that a decision-taker regards a threat to the club as a threat to himself and that the club's revenue (the membership fees of the other members) D is fixed, the boundary of the club's extinction zone is B and the decision-taker has income d and subsistence level b. The decision-taker provides the club with an amount a from his income. The probability of simultaneous economic survival of the individual and the club is

111 See, for example, Buchanan, J. M.: An Economic Theory of Clubs. *Economica* 32, 125(1965): 1–14, and also Frohlich, N., Hunt, T., Oppenheimer, J., Wagner, R. H.: Individual Contributions for Collective Goods: Alternative Models. *The Journal of Conflict Resolution* 19, 2(1975): 310–29, and Hart, J. A., Cowhey, P. F.: Theories of Collective Goods Reexamined. *The Western Political Quarterly* 30, 3(1977): 351–62.

112 Hayek, F. A. von: *The Road to Serfdom.* Chicago: University of Chicago Press, 2007 (first published in 1944).

113 See Heller, M. A.: The Tragedy of the Anticommons. Property in the Transition from Marx to Markets. *Harvard Law Review* 111, 3(1998): 621–88, or Buchanan, J. M., Yoon, Y. J.: Symmetric Tragedies: Commons and Anticommons. *Journal of Law and Economics* 43, 1(2000): 1–14.

114 See Veblen, T.: *The Theory of the Leisure Class: An Economic Study of Institutions.* New York: Macmillan, 1899, pp. 68–101.

$$p(a) = \frac{d-b-a}{d-a} \cdot \frac{D-B+a}{D+a} = \left(1 - \frac{b}{d-a}\right)\left(1 - \frac{B}{D+a}\right).$$

We are seeking the optimum, so we set the first derivative equal to zero:

$$p'(a) = \frac{b}{(d-a)^2} \cdot \left(1 - \frac{B}{D+a}\right) - \frac{B}{(D+a)^2} \cdot \left(1 - \frac{b}{d-a}\right) = 0.$$

The domain of function $p'(a)$ is the semi-closed interval $\langle 0, d-b)$, since we cannot expect the provision of a subsidy that is 100% self-destructive.

Let us assume that the extinction threat to the individual is lower than the threat to the club (otherwise the decision-taker is more threatened and it is irrational for him to pay any membership fee to the club):

$$\frac{d-b}{d} > \frac{D-B}{D}, \text{ i.e. } \frac{b}{d} < \frac{B}{D}.$$

Given this assumption, function $p'(a)$ has values with the opposite sign at the extreme points of its domain:

$$p'(0) = \frac{b}{d^2} \cdot \left(1 - \frac{B}{D}\right) - \frac{B}{D^2} \cdot \left(1 - \frac{b}{d}\right) > 0,$$

$$p'(d-b) = \frac{b}{d^2} \cdot \left(1 - \frac{B}{D+d-b}\right) < 0.$$

Hence, given that $p'(a)$ is continuous, there must be a root of equation $p'(a) = 0$ that is the member's optimal membership fee. Given the decreasing shape of function $p'(a)$ (because, as can be demonstrated, $p''(a) < 0$ over the entire domain, hence function $p(a)$ is strictly concave), there is just one root and so the optimal membership fee a^* given parameters b, d, B and D is unique.

For illustration, Figure 61 plots $p(a)$ for the case where $d = 3, D = 2, b = B = 1$. The optimal membership fee here is $a^* = 0.5$.

It is worth noting that under the given conditions the membership fees of the individual members are not equal, i.e. each member has a different optimal membership fee. However, this ceases to hold if we abandon the assumption that the membership fees of all agents except the decision-taker are given. In this case we arrive at a much more complex problem where we need to combine the approaches of generalized microeconomics and game theory. We will consider the possibilities of these approaches in future research.

Figure 61: The probability of simultaneous survival of the individual and the club versus the individual membership fee

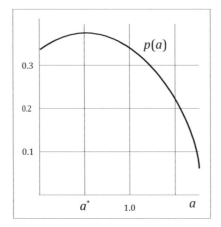

10.2.1.5 MUTUALITY (SOLIDARITY) OF COMMUNITY MEMBERS

A sense of belonging to the community makes an individual willing to make sacrifices to eliminate external threats, be they through degeneration of the community or through a threat to the community from outside. He may do this out of simple fear or out of feeling for the community (environmentalists speak of the "principle of collective guilt" that a growing proportion of the population shares regarding the environment).

Mutuality manifests itself, for example, as:

- an effort to prevent the community (e.g. a firm, a family, a club or an informal group of collaborating firms) from collapsing,
- an urge not to damage the environment or opposition to the misuse of science due to the fear of human extinction,
- a willingness to sacrifice part of one's prosperity to educate "one's own" doctors and other educated people,
- a willingness to support the strengthening of the community against external enemies (support for the army) or against internal freeloaders (support for the police).

The urge to protect the community can be explained by the urge for cooperative, social behaviour that has arisen during human evolution. The collective utility strategy here can also be explained in terms of the biological mechanisms through which an individual subordinates himself to the majority or to the strongest individuals in a hostile world and in difficult situations.

Such evolution, however, can also result in a "moral imperative". To explain this, we need to take into account a far broader range of causes of mutuality, including upbringing, value systems and respect for truth and freedom.

It has been demonstrated that people (individuals) in smaller communities behave more considerately, decently, helpfully and cooperatively. Their willingness to work together and help each other, including by redistributing individual wealth among members of the community, is also higher.[115]

We will present additional models of altruistic behaviour and belonging to the community based on generalized microeconomics in section 10.3.

10.2.1.6 RESPECT FOR AUTHORITY

Since prehistoric times, the fight for survival has led people in the majority to accept and welcome a social contract with an authority (e.g. a tribal leader or the state). In return for its position of supremacy, this authority provides others with the ability to organize resistance against external and internal threats. Under this contract, people expect the ruler to prevent mutual wrongs by means of penalties and to encourage cohesive behaviour by means of rewards. The authority defines the space for "fair" individual competition, thereby allowing people to benefit from trade in the market. The authority makes life more secure and more predictable.

One of the elements of respect for authority (and in recent decades perhaps one of its main elements) is respect for the media, especially television. Surprisingly, even the better educated classes of society regard instructions emanating from the television as a benchmark of values and behaviour. People often stop conducting their own analysis and incline to believe "proven" opinions. The louder the voice, the stronger the inclination. If the opinions promoted on television include the need to pay taxes or make donations, the social acceptability of redistribution can be positively affected. If, on the other hand, voices on television condemn the unemployed as workshy, people's willingness to cede part of their earnings to others will fall sharply.

People's inclination towards authority and their willingness to give up part of their prosperity to it of course rise at times of change, at times when a sense of uncertainty and threat dominates. At such times, people are willing to pay a premium for security.

A specific feature here from the microeconomic perspective is the hierarchical structure of decision-taking and the dual assessment of an agent's economic situation (his own and that of the authority above him). Sections 10.3 and 10.4 contain hierarchical models based on generalized microeconomics.

---

115 See Milgram, S.: The Experience of Living in Cities. *Science* 167, 3924(1970): 1461–68.

10.2.2 THE WILLINGNESS TO REDISTRIBUTE IN FAVOUR OF PUBLIC GOODS (THE ACCEPTABILITY OF TAXATION)

Another reason we can identify for forming communities is the common public interest, which can include the acquisition and operation of public goods (positive externalities).

The main problem with public goods is the deviousness (pragmatism) of Olson's "free rider", who tries to benefit from public goods without helping to pay for them.[116] Free riders endanger the production of a necessary public good by reducing the general level of mutuality and people's willingness to sacrifice their own prosperity for the benefit of the community. The size of the community also reduces this willingness—the larger the group, the harder it is (*ceteris paribus*) to ensure that a public good is produced; conversely, the smaller the group of individuals with a common interest, the greater the probability of collective action.[117] If the individual costs are too high, the externality and the related community do not even come into existence. Olson refers to such communities as latent groups.

From his deliberations about the notorious free rider, Olson concludes that a condition for the existence of large groups is that a small group inside this large group must have the opportunity to gain a bigger share of the benefits arising from organizing the production of public goods. There need to be selective incentives for individuals to work for the group's interest (e.g. the high prestige of the corresponding public office, satisfaction of the ambition to hold power).

Small groups and organizations are necessarily more effective in achieving their goals. The larger such communities are, the lower are the per-person costs associated with public goods, but the more opportunities there are for free riding. In addition, large groups are also easily subject to "asset stripping" by well-organized subgroups, which can gain a privileged position in large groups. Alongside free riding, this "oligarchization"—the formation of privileged groups within a community having a fixed management hierarchy—is the second important factor of destruction of mutuality, especially in large communities.

If a shared public interest (shaping the community's identity) and potential collective action (strengthening the community's identity) are sufficiently attractive, they help to shape a collective identity (perceived mutuality) and foster a prevailing departure from the purely egoistic interest of individuals. The acceptability of redistribution to the individual is strengthened.

---

116 See Olson, M.: *The Logic of Collective Action. Public Goods and the Theory of Groups.* Cambridge, MA: Harvard University Press, 1965.

117 This applies to all public goods except for security; for externalities of a security nature the opposite tends to be true.

Although it is possible to model such preferences using generalized micro-economics, it is difficult to interpret the extinction zone of the public economy. When applying the model of maximization of the Pareto probability of survival in this way, we need to treat the boundary of the extinction zone as the limit beyond which public finances—in the opinion of the economic agent whose decision-making we are modelling—will collapse. The problem is, however, that for each agent this boundary is in a different place. Consequently, we have to model the tax-evading free rider in one way and the responsible taxpayer in another.

The aforementioned classification of the motives for altruistic behaviour and for the willingness to give up one's own prosperity in the context of redistribution is not disjunctive, as a combination of several types of motives is often present.

Based on the preceding considerations and on our own experience, we will formulate several (certainly debatable) hypotheses relating to the willingness to pay various types of tax. We argue that taxes that are beneficial to the economic survival (economic prosperity) of a community which we feel part of and whose welfare is integral to our personal welfare or whose extinction would be a great personal loss to us, are acceptable.

10.2.3 HYPOTHESES REGARDING THE WILLINGNESS TO CONTRIBUTE TO REDISTRIBUTION

H1: The willingness to redistribute on the basis of hard-core altruism is greater when the assistance is well targeted, preferably at ensuring the survival of a specific person or a worthy institution whose demise would represent a personal loss.

H2: Reciprocal altruism derivable from personal mutuality has a place primarily in intergenerational support in old age. However, there is a risk here of free-riding. More rigorous separation of pension benefits and maintenance of strict state control would increase the acceptability of this (de facto tax) payment, as it might then be better understood as provision for one's own economic survival.

H3: People's inclination toward authority and their willingness to give up part of their prosperity to it rise at times when a sense of uncertainty and threat dominates. The stronger the authority, the more acceptable this type of redistribution is. Greater willingness to pay these taxes is displayed by wealthier individuals, as they are more concerned about their property, and, in extremely poor countries, by the poor, who are concerned about their own physical survival.

H4: People in smaller communities behave more considerately and coopera-tively and are more willing to redistribute wealth among members of the com-munity. As a result, local (e.g. municipal) taxes are more acceptable to taxpay-ers, as they provide for the survival of a closer community, i.e. a more significant element of one's personal "me".

H5: Knowledge of the opportunities to deceive and abuse others for one's own benefit increases hand in hand with growth in the benefits of mutual coopera-tion. High acceptability of taxation is conditional on the elimination of free rid-ers and of the scope for their free rides, which threaten the economic survival of the community and therefore reduce people's willingness to pay taxes.

H6: People prefer their money to be used in well-targeted ways and therefore prefer assigned taxes, where they get a say in how the money collected is spent.

H7: People are often irrational when it comes to taxes. In sociological studies, they regard progressive direct taxation (a higher tax rate on higher income) as fairer than taxation hidden in the price (VAT, excise duty). *Ceteris paribus*, however, the latter tends to be identified by taxpayers as a smaller perceived loss than income tax.

The following table tries to characterize the aforementioned hypotheses and identify the individual types of motives to pay/accept various forms of tax.

Table 7: Identification of taxpayers' motives to accept taxes

motive type of tax	leaning on authority	reciprocal altruism	interest of the state	interest of the municipality	free riders
excise duty			yes		
property tax (local)			yes	yes	yes
income tax	yes				yes
pension insurance		yes			
health insurance		yes			

After verifying and supplementing these hypotheses regarding taxpayers' mo-tives for accepting individual types of tax, it would be possible to find a micro-economic starting point for thinking about the appropriate shares of individual taxes in taxpayers' budgets and thus get a handle on the supply side of redistri-bution. What we have here is a noteworthy area of common interest between economics and sociology.

10.2.4 THE "DEMAND SIDE" OF REDISTRIBUTION:
THE INFORMATION PROBLEM

Deliberate distortion of information is a problem with any allocation of resources where a higher authority has decision-making powers. If the welfare
or even survival of agents is dependent on allocations "from above", the information they provide cannot usually be trusted. Wealth-maximizing agents will
distort information in such a way as to maximize their own benefit.

This was proven true by the functioning of communist centrally planned
economies (CPEs). Even in a market economy, where (unlike in a CPE) agents
can ultimately cease to be, one has to assume that a large proportion of agents
will, in a crisis, try to reduce (minimize) their probability of extinction by deliberately distorting information.

The danger of deliberate information distortion by information providers
was identified as an information problem in CPEs, and possible methods for at
least partially eliminating such deliberate distortions were discussed.[118] These
methods included the following:

A. Concentrating on information that incentivizes information objectivity, in the sense that distorting such information is disadvantageous for
providers (reduces their individual prosperity).
B. Decomposing the system so that the synchronization of criteria at individual hierarchical levels is enhanced by the obligation for central authorities to be involved at lower levels of the hierarchy (e.g. at local level).
C. Giving greater weight to agents that behave unselfishly.

A: Information flows that incentivize information objectivity

Certain types of information give agents an incentive to tell the truth. With such
information, providers of false information are automatically economically pe-
nalized so severely that it does not pay them to be dishonest.

Information flows from producers to a higher (central) authority usually
contain information about:

- production capacity, especially in relation to subsidies granted,
- production plans, especially investment and innovation plans, and ways
of increasing exports,
- optimal workforce size,
- emissions reductions through the use of greener technology.

---

118 The information problem is formulated, and possible ways in which the central authority can incentivize the provision of undistorted information for CPEs is assessed, in Hlaváček, J.: *Objektivizace informací
v plánovacím dialogu—možnosti a meze*. Praha: Academia, 1989, and Kotulan, A.: Konstrukce stimulační
funkce indukující nezkreslené informace. *Politická ekonomie* 32, 2(1984): 250–65.

The essence of incentivizing information objectivity is to set multiple constraints and allow the subsidy recipient to reduce the strictness of one condition at the expense of another (referred to in centrally planned economies as "substitution of the strictness of plan constraints", or "accommodative planning"[119]).

These options, which were originally considered during unsuccessful attempts to make centrally planned economies more efficient, also exist in market economies despite their fundamentally different economic conditions. Such economies have multi-source financing, with substitution of strictness of conditions for entitlement to individual partial subsidies.

Another possibility is to rigorously consider the agent's "subsidy history", i.e. to threaten to turn off the central subsidy tap in the future if the recipient makes empty promises.

The complexity of the information problem in the provision of central support to producers consists in the fact that we have to work with two criteria in the set of feasible solutions of each agent seeking a redistributive subsidy: the criterion of the subsidy recipient and the criterion of the donor, or central authority, distributing resources among multiple agents. Generalized economics offers a suitable modelling toolkit for doing so.

B: Decomposition of the system

The information superiority of the subsidy recipient over the central authority decreases with decreasing distance of the authority to the recipient. On the other hand, the more local authorities there are, or the more complicated their hierarchical structure is, the more difficult it is to coordinate redistribution.

The information problem of redistribution (the threat of intentional distortion of information by a subsidy recipient) can be partially reduced by establishing an appropriate hierarchical structure for the redistribution process. This will allow:

- more efficient use of resources by permitting a higher-level authority to make its subsidies conditional on the involvement of a lower-level authority that has a better knowledge of the recipients of redistributed resources,
- the setting of subsidy limits for agents in a subsystem managed by a local authority,
- control of lower levels by optimally empowered higher levels in the hierarchical structure of the redistribution process (optimal in the sense

---

119 This was a purely theoretical concept, a procedure which did not and could not work in the anti-efficient climate of central planning. See Hlaváček, J.: *Objektivizace informací v plánovacím dialogu—možnosti a meze.* Praha: Academia, 1989, pp. 128–30.

that the higher level must not have strong enough powers to excessively restrict the local authority's freedom to make decisions).

C: Giving greater weight to agents that behave unselfishly

Giving greater weight to agents that behave unselfishly in the economy obviously reduces the problem of intentional distortion of information, regardless of whether such unselfish behaviour is motivated by:

- fear of compromising the goodwill of the firm and thereby reducing the prosperity of the potential subsidy recipient,
- respect for authority, for example a professional community,
- the agent's interest in enhancing the strength or quality of the community as a whole,
- a shared interest leading to shared consumption of public or community (club) goods.

Here again, it holds that under certain conditions, being trustworthy (including not yielding to the temptation to make easy money by distorting information) can pay in terms of an agent's material interests. This is a special case of the parable of the hawk and the dove.[120]

10.2.5 EFFICIENCY OF REDISTRIBUTION IN RELATION TO THE DONOR'S PREFERENCES

Let us now try to identify the main factors which motivate a donor to provide support and which also affect the amount and allocation of that support.

A. Economic benefit of the weakest links

Redistribution from the economically strong to the economically weak need not always come at the cost of the efficiency of the economy as a whole. It is not unusual for the marginal product of a resource (the deciding factor as regards allocation efficiency) to be higher for an agent that is economically threatened. This can give rise to a situation where redistribution increases the economic efficiency of a community (for example the economy as a whole). This can happen, for example:

- in small firms as a result of monopsonistic retail chains preferring large suppliers,

---

120 See Frank, R. H.: *Microeconomics and Behavior.* New York: McGraw-Hill, 2006, pp. 236–39. In terms of the probability of personal survival it is better under certain conditions to be a cooperative and truthful "dove" than a selfish and thoughtless "hawk".

- as a result of threats due to external factors (arising outside the market environment of the economy), e.g. crop failure, panicking customers, import barriers introduced in other countries,
- in the short term in underfunded firms with high potential,
- as a result of one group of firms being at a relative disadvantage, for example because they have worse access to credit or because politically motivated or corrupt decisions made by the state or municipality have put their competitors at an advantage.

In all these cases, purely market allocation is sub-optimal because the market environment has been significantly disrupted. Here, levelling the playing field (primarily for individual agents on the market) via redistribution is a way to achieve optimal allocation in the long term.

In all other cases, redistribution is accompanied by a reduction in allocation efficiency and must be justified by the "trade-off" argument. Is it worth sacrificing part of attainable production or saveable resources in the interests of the state (armament, food self-sufficiency, regional support)?

B. Maintaining the existing structure or attaining the desired one

Allocation in favour of the weakest links may also, of course, be a result of purely economic calculation by the central authority. If resources are being allocated to maintaining the existing structure or attaining the desired structure in the economic system, it is optimal to support weak links that in this case represent "bottlenecks" to growth of society in the desired structure. The optimal redistribution, therefore, is allocation that is indirectly proportional to the marginal product, i.e. an agent that is capable of achieving a four-times higher increase in the value of one more unit of a resource than another agent gets a four-times lower allocation. This is the source of the comparative advantage stemming from foreign trade and also of the foresightedness[121] of the post-Velvet Revolution Czech privatization path, which involved no prior restructuring.

The very inclusion of a formulation of the desired (sectoral or regional) production structure in redistribution schemes therefore always greatly reduces the efficiency of allocation or redistribution. Although it may not seem more "economical" to the public, it is more rational to derive the level of support for the regions from their needs and not to justify and quantify this redistribution on the basis of a "desirable", centrally determined (sectoral or regional) structure of the economic system as a whole.

---

121 We choose the term "foresightedness" despite the currently prevailing criticism of the Czech privatization path. Poor results are no guarantee that any other path would not have been significantly more disadvantageous or unviable.

C. Averting threats to the community

Redistribution is most frequently a manifestation of solidarity with the community and its members. To model it, we need to describe behaviour within the community. This will allow us to analyse how the behaviour of the community as a whole can be derived from individual preferences containing solidarity with the community. It is appropriate to distinguish between *Gemeinschaft* (community) and *Gesellschaft* (society):

C1. Threats to Gemeinschaft.

In this case, coexistence is ordained by meaning (and not justified by purpose and the benefit for members[122]). Examples include families, groups of friends, familial communities and even local communities.

In *Gemeinschaften*, the manifestations of incorporation of the interests of the community into those of the individual (on the economic level) can include:

- an altruistically motivated membership contribution to common funds,
- support provided to needy community members with no expectation of reciprocity,
- gratuitous support and preferential treatment given to community members,[123]
- a willingness to die defending the community.

The point of redistribution can be assessed even for *Gemeinschaften*. The criterion (of Darwinian type, i.e. maximization of the probability of survival of the individual or the community) is survival—not only the biological survival of the individual or the community, but also, for instance, the survival of the state as a democratic society without serious social upheaval or the economic survival of a family without collapse. In models for describing the behaviour of individuals in *Gemeinschaften*, one can derive the dependence of the optimal allocation of resources (from the survival point of view) on the total income of the community. In some cases, it is optimal to sacrifice a member of the community (altruism can be cruel[124]).

C2. Threats to Gesellschaft

Gesellschaft is justified by purpose and the benefit for members. A *Gesellschaft* member views a threat to the community as a loss, although only to the ex-

---

122 Even in Gemeinschaften, a special purpose can prevail—a group of friends can turn into a criminal gang and a family can turn into an economic unit earning in order to consume conspicuously or conversely into an environment for caring for a disabled child. Here, however, purpose is derived from meaning. Hence, the nature of the community is unchanged, as the original meaning is unaltered.

123 As we argued above, mutuality is no guarantee of morality. Giving preferential treatment to a creditor is a criminal offence that in mature democracies is viewed as being equally repellent as fraud and theft.

124 See Hlaváček, J., Hlaváček, M.: Cruel Altruism. *Prague Economic Papers* 14, 4(2005): 363–71.

tent that the loss does not exceed the benefit he derives from his membership. The most common economic *Gesellschaften* are firms, cartels, non-profit sports clubs and other non-profit organizations.

The manifestations of *Gesellschaft* mutuality (the willingness to redistribute in favour of other members or in favour of the community as a whole) include:

- support for the society to which you belong, but which you regard merely as a means of acquiring status or making money,
- contribution to common funds motivated by the potential individual financial loss associated with the potential downfall of the community,
- a guarantee vis-à-vis third-parties motivated by expected reciprocity.

For this type of community we can assume that for each member there is a relatively constant amount representing the individual's perceived value of membership. In contrast to *Gemeinschaft*, where the individual regards joint consumption as part of his own consumption, in *Gesellschaft* every reduction in individual consumption is perceived as a loss and is compared with the value of membership. If the perceived loss is greater than the value of membership, the individual leaves and regards his departure as a gain rather than a loss. The individual's departure can often reduce the value of membership for other individuals and can set off a chain of events leading very rapidly to the collapse of the community.

Gesellschaften always have an administrator of common resources (a common budget). We refer to him as the decision-taker, although he is not necessarily an authoritative "ruler" of the community who can ignore others when making his decisions. The models for describing individuals' behaviour in economic *Gesellschaften* deal, for example, with the situation where the decision-taker (the administrator of the common budget) can, by providing his support, save only some parts of the community and condemn the rest to extinction (for example by not supporting them). Here again, the optimal allocation of shared resources also depends fundamentally on the decision-taker's criterion function (preferences). Sometimes it is optimal to divide up a subsidy equally, but other times it is optimal to prefer the most sensitively reacting member and, once that member's survival has been 100% guaranteed, to redirect the support to the next (second most sensitively reacting) individual. The optimal allocation also sometimes depends fundamentally on the relations between the parameters determining the agents' threat zone boundaries.

In the previous research phase[125] several common budget models were derived for a two-member community (for example a partnership). The common budget is split into three parts—two parts for satisfying the individual needs

---

125 Culminating in Hlaváček, J., et al.: *Mikroekonomie sounáležitosti se společenstvím*. Praha: Karolinum, 1999.

of the two members of the community and the remainder for providing for the running of the community as a whole. We assumed that there is a community leader who draws up the common budget and decides on the allocation of resources. This decision-taker perceives three threats:

- the threat of insufficient resources to satisfy his individual needs,
- the threat of insufficient resources to satisfy his partner's needs,
- the threat of insufficient resources for the community as a whole.

If we assume very simplistically that the individual threats are independent, the decision-taker's optimum, i.e. the point of maximum probability of (economic) survival, lies within the set of feasible situations. It turns out that the larger part of any additional income will go to the community member who convinces the other one that he faces the greater threat. In other words, modesty can worsen one's economic position in the community, the more so the lower the total resources for the community. We can also interpret this as the model of a family that has degenerated into *Gesellschaft* (in order to increase the prosperity of its members).

We distinguish three criteria: egoistic, altruistic and symmetric. A comparison of the individual models reveals that

- the optimal allocation always lies within the set of feasible situations,[126]
- the funds earmarked for the community (family) as a whole are largest when there is a dominant altruist and smallest in the symmetric situation,
- the greatest inequality in the degree of satisfaction of individual needs occurs in the dominant altruist case.

If we abandon the decision-taker's criterion and look at all three cases from the perspective an independent observer (weighing the risk of collapse of an altruist close to boundary of biological survival) a family with a dominant (but self-threatening) altruist would (paradoxically?) be an extremely endangered community.

The rules of redistribution, in the sense of achieving the purpose of redistribution (which can be mere survival) are not trivial. Optimal redistribution depends not only on decision-taker's criterion regarding shared resources, but also on the amount of those resources. There is a discontinuity (unusual in standard microeconomics) where a marginal change (for example in the donor's income) leads to a fundamental change in the optimal allocation (redistribution) strategy. We will demonstrate this in section 10.3.2.

---

126 This is unusual: in standard microeconomics, based on decision-making problems in the form of maximization of profit or other utility subject to a given set of constraints, the optimum (in the deterministic case) lies on the boundary of the set of feasible solutions. See Chapter 1.

10.3 ALTRUISTIC ALLOCATION MODELS

If the assumed individual criterion of a rational donor-altruist is his probability of (economic) survival inclusive of his community memberships, the degree (intensity) of his sense of belonging manifests itself in his decision-making problem as the relative magnitude of his aversion to situations threatening the survival of community members or of the community as a whole. By "relative" here we mean relative to the magnitude of his aversion to situations threatening the survival of the individual himself. A greater sense of belonging to a given community compared to other communities does not necessarily mean that the individual will leave them sooner: it depends on the situation and on the set of feasible solutions to his decision-making problem. A greater sense of belonging to a given community means that leaving that community represents a greater relative loss (relative to other communities) for the individual, which, however, the individual can be forced into by the situation. Therefore, we do not adopt Hirschman's term "loyalty" but use the term "sense of belonging": an individual can (at a given moment in time and under the pressure of circumstance) cease to be loyal to a community but still have an intense feeling for it and perceive his non-membership as a loss (one that will allow him to avoid a greater loss). Belonging is a matter of individual preferences, whereas loyalty is a matter of individual behaviour.[127]

Individuals with a feeling of belonging do not, of course, set their own interests and the interests of the community against each other (like an egoist), but rather set them side by side. They seek a decision that will support the simultaneous survival of themselves and the community or those close to them. They therefore behave altruistically—to the detriment of their own prosperity they provide resources to other individuals who are members of the community or whom they regard as members of the community, be it a formal or an informal one.

In the following text we will give several examples of models of altruism where a rational altruist (donor, sponsor) provides a financial subsidy to recipients and thereby reduces their threat of extinction at the cost of a threat to

---

127 We can illustrate this using the situational risk aversion model in Hlaváček, J., et al.: *Mikroekonomie sounáležitosti se společenstvím*. Praha: Karolinum, 1999, pp. 176–82. An entrepreneur who feels himself to be member of a community of trustworthy (not excessive risk-taking) individuals is forced by the pressure of circumstances (in the interests of maximizing his probability of survival) to renounce his membership of that community and embark on a high-risk project (which offers him at least some chance of survival). He may perceive this as a greater loss than quitting the community of entrepreneurs, but the latter would not increase his probability of survival. His sense of belonging (the weight of the community in the individual's criterion) is higher with regard to the first community (trustworthy individuals), but the individual nevertheless (as a result of a particular situation, i.e. a particular set of feasible solutions to his decision-making problem) remains loyal to the second community (the association of entrepreneurs).

himself. We will show how the optimum amount of a gift (subsidy) provided to a supported individual or the optimum allocation of a subsidy to individual recipients changes fundamentally depending on the criterion of the donor.

We assume that survival depends exclusively on income and we will again work with the first-order Pareto distribution, which displays zero probability for income at the survival zone boundary and a probability converging to one as income tends to infinity. The symbols used have the following meanings:

b_0 the extinction zone boundary of the donor,
b_1 the extinction zone boundary of the recipient,
a the amount of the subsidy,
d the donor's income before implementing the subsidy.

We assume that the recipient has no income before the subsidy is implemented. We therefore assume for simplicity that the subsidy a is his only income.

By applying the first-order Pareto distribution to the survival probabilities of the two individuals under consideration[128] we obtain:

$$p_0(d) = 0 \qquad \text{for} \quad d - a < b_0,$$

$$= \frac{d-a-b_0}{d-a} \qquad \text{for} \quad d - a \geq b_0,$$

$$p_1(d) = 0 \qquad \text{for} \quad a < b_1,$$

$$= \frac{a-b_1}{a} \qquad \text{for} \quad a \geq b_1.$$

10.3.1 MODEL OF ABSOLUTE SOLIDARITY

In this model, the criterion of a rational donor is maximization of the probability of simultaneous survival of the recipient and the donor, which is given by the product of their probabilities of survival.

Therefore, the donor here assesses the threat to himself as being equal to the threat to the recipient. We assume that the sole threat to both individuals is a low amount of funds.

In this case, the donor's criterion when deciding on the subsidy amount is the following function:

$$p(a) = \frac{d-a-b_0}{d-a} \cdot \frac{a-b_1}{a},$$

---

128 See section 1.3.1.

where the initial income d and the extinction zone boundaries b_0 and b_1 are parameters of the problem

$$a^* = \arg \max p(a).$$

Suppose that the donor has enough income to ensure the survival of both individuals:

$$d > b_0 + b_1.$$

We fix parameters b_0 and b_1 and introduce function $a(d)$, which gives the optimal subsidy as a function of the initial income. The domain of this function is the interval $(b_0 + b_1, +\infty)$.

If the two agents have the same extinction zone boundary, i.e. if $b_0 = b_1$, the optimal strategy is obviously equal distribution of income between the two agents:[129]

$$a(d) = \frac{d}{2}.$$

Figure 62: The subsidy amount versus the donor's initial income d_0 in the absolute solidarity model where the two individuals are equally resilient ($b_0 = b_1$)

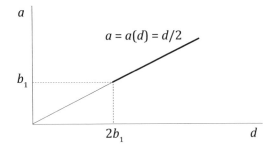

If $b_0 \neq b_1$, the solution to the problem is to prefer the more threatened individual. The following two figures show the subsidy amount as a function of the donor's initial income. In Figure 63 the recipient is more resilient, while in Figure 64 the donor is more resilient.

---

129 At the optimum it must hold that the marginal transfer of funds from the first agent to the second will reduce the latter's probability of extinction to an equal extent as it increases the former's probability of extinction. In other words, the derivatives of the probability of extinction with respect to the amount of funds obtained must be equal. From this we can derive the optimal ratio in which the donor divides disposable income d.

Figure 63: The subsidy amount versus the donor's initial income d_0 in the absolute solidarity model where the recipient is more resilient ($b_0 < b_1$).

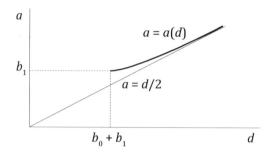

Figure 64: The subsidy amount versus the donor's initial income d_0 in the absolute solidarity model where the donor is more resilient ($b_0 > b_1$).

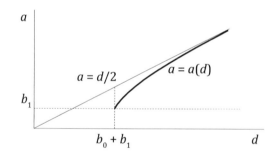

Logically, therefore, the donor's behaviour is determined not only by the specific altruistic criterion, but also by the situation of each individual (in our case specifically by their relative resilience or threat of extinction, i.e. by the relationship between parameters b_0 and b_1). In some situations the donor will strongly prefer himself, but in other situations he is capable of increasing his own personal threat of extinction by providing a subsidy.

10.3.2 MODEL OF MINIMIZATION OF THE RISK OF SIMULTANEOUS EXTINCTION OF BOTH INDIVIDUALS: CRUEL ALTRUISM

In this model, the donor maximizes the probability of survival of at least one (any) member of the community. This probability can be expressed as follows:

[donor's survival probability] + [recipient's survival probability] –

– [probability of simultaneous survival of both agents]:[130]

$$p(a) = \frac{d-a-b_0}{d-a} + \frac{a-b_1}{a} - \frac{d-a-b_0}{d-a} \cdot \frac{a-b_1}{a}.$$

Suppose that the donor has enough income to ensure the survival of at least one of the two agents:

$d > \min (b_0, b_1).$

In this case, we again model the donor's decision by the optimization

$a^* = \arg \max p(a),$

where the domain of function $a(d)$ (which gives the optimal subsidy as a function of initial income given the fixed extinction zone boundaries) is this time the interval $(\min (b_0, b_1), +\infty)$.

The donor has two possible strategies and will choose the most advantageous with respect to the probability of survival of at least one agent:

      Strategy I: ensure that the more resilient agent survives and the less resilient one does not (by not providing a subsidy),

      Strategy II: ensure that both agents survive.

If the two agents have the same subsistence level, i.e. if $b_0 = b_1 = b$, the donor will have to choose which agent (out of the two equally resilient ones) will survive. Suppose that the recipient will be the survivor. For income $d \le 2b$ the donor will leave his entire income to the recipient and will die himself, because such a low income is insufficient to ensure the survival (with a non-zero probability) of both agents. He will therefore, of course, choose Strategy I:

$a(d) = d$ for $d \le 2b.$

However, even if the donor's income d allows for the simultaneous survival of both members, i.e. if $d > 2b$, Strategy I may be more advantageous because it will provide a higher probability of survival of at least one agent. This will be the case for a lower-than-boundary income level, which in our case is four times the extinction zone boundary $d_h = 4b$. At this boundary income level, the

---

maximized probability is the same for both strategies (we denote the probability of survival of at least one agent for Strategy I and income d by $p^I(d)$ and the same for Strategy II by $p^{II}(d)$):

$$p^I(4b) = \frac{4b-b}{4b} = \frac{3}{4} = p^{II}(4b) = 2 \cdot \frac{2b-b}{2b} - \left(\frac{2b-b}{2b}\right)^2.$$

The donor prefers Strategy I if income is below the boundary level (i.e. if $d \le d_h$). If it is above this level (i.e. if $d > d_h$) the donor's optimal strategy is fundamentally different. Instead of providing equal support to both, he will transfer all funds to a selected member. At the boundary point, the path of the optimum is discontinuous:

$$\lim_{d \to d_h+} a(d) \ne \lim_{d \to d_h-} a(d).$$

Figure 65 shows the subsidy amount as a function of the donor's initial income for the case where $b_0 = b_1 = b$:

Figure 65: The optimal subsidy a versus the donor's income d in the model of minimization of the risk of simultaneous extinction of both agents—the case of equally threatened agents; below the boundary income level d_h the donor sacrifices himself

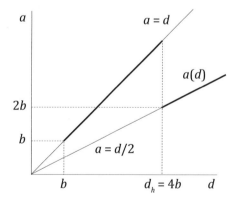

If the two individuals are equally resilient and, by contrast, the recipient is sacrificed, the optimal subsidy path $a(d)$ changes only in that the subsidy is zero when income is below the boundary level:

Figure 66: Ditto with the recipient being sacrificed below the boundary income level

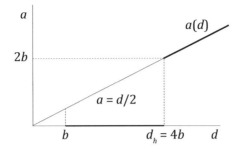

If the donor is the more resilient, i.e. if $b_0 < b_1$, the plot of the optimal subsidy a against income d is similar as in the previous figure, the only difference being that the boundary point moves to the right, i.e. the switch to Strategy II occurs at higher income d. We illustrate this in Figure 67 for the case where $b_0 = b$ and $b_1 = 2b$.

Figure 67: Ditto for the case where the recipient is more threatened

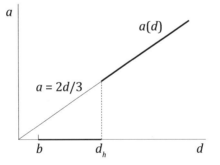

When trying to minimize the risk of extinction of both agents, a rational donor will therefore behave discontinuously at the boundary[131] point $d_h = 9b$. If his income falls, say, from level $d = 10b$, there will be a sudden and drastic change in his behaviour at level $d = 9b$ and his originally totally altruistic transfer of two-thirds of his income will change: the donor (according to the logic of the assumed criteria of maximization of the probability of survival of at least one agent) will completely stop providing the subsidy, thereby condemning the subsidized agent to death.

---

131 As in the previous case, the probability of survival of at least one agent at the boundary point $d = 9b$ is the same for Strategies I and II: $p^I(9b) = p^{II}(9b) = 8/9$. For $d < 9b$ Strategy I is better, while for $d > 9b$ Strategy II is better.

10.4 THE STATE IN THE ROLE OF DONOR[132]

Economics is the science of rational allocation of resources. This allocation, however, involves redistribution (in particular by the state). Almost half the income in the advanced economies is redistributed. The proportion of redistributed income has been rising fairly rapidly (along with the tax rate) since the start of the 20th century owing to the constantly rising importance of public goods and social services.

Consequently, public goods (positive externalities) and social services are not and cannot be the result of market forces and decisions alone. For example, vital social services may fail to be provided because the low income of those who receive them makes them unprofitable. Likewise, a shortage of public goods can represent a bottleneck in an economy and thwart profitable activity. For example, an inability to stop free riders consuming public goods makes it impossible to cover the costs by collecting payments from users (people don't normally pay if they don't have to). As a result, it is the state that always takes responsibility for public goods and social services. This does not mean, however, that the state provides these services directly itself—it has proven more efficient to provide state subsidies to private providers of such goods.

The inclusion of redistribution does not mean we have to abandon the idea of assessing the economic rationality of resource allocation. As we argued in the introduction to this section, the fact that social services and public goods are not fully determined by market forces does not mean we are getting outside the realm of economics. Even state subsidies can be provided economically rationally and economically irrationally. State subsidy allocation rules may or may not create bottlenecks, unnecessary expenses, scope for corruption and so on. An economically rational state (with sensible rules) can achieve the same effect at lower cost than an irrational state.

The issue of providing support is unquestionably an economic problem, even if in some cases (the hard-core altruism of a private donor) it lies outside the *homo economicus* paradigm. Yet although the motives of a private donor can be either (economically irrationally) altruistic or self-interested (e.g. corporate image building), a donor that is part of the public economy acts in the public interest (provided he stays within the bounds of the law). Such a donor is most often the state, but it can also be a local authority or an international organization providing aid to developing or third world economies. We limit ourselves here to the case where the state is the guardian of the public interest.

The motive of the state in the role of donor for public service providers is itself a problem. One possible approach is to assume that the state minimizes the amount of public funds it needs to provide in order to ensure that its citizens

---

132 See Hlaváček, J., Hlaváček, M.: Ekonomická iracionalita donátora plynoucí z nedůvěry k příjemci dotace. *Finance a úvěr* 54, 3–4(2004): 138–54.

live a dignified life and in order to safeguard the economic survival of the sector of the economy which provides public goods and services. It redistributes funds, primarily from taxes, to the needy and the dependent and to selected firms. In the case of firms, however, there are two problems. The state does not know the threshold (different for different firms) below which a subsidized entity will collapse. It is also debatable to assume that the state prefers a situation where all public service providers scrape along at the very edge of survival and a high percentage of them go under.[133]

If the donor (state) is to distribute subsidies in an economically rational way, it must try to secure the maximum possible return on the funds provided for the public or social services or other activities performed by the recipient. It can distribute funds among the recipients in basically two ways. The first is to provide funds in proportion to the proven (justified) needs of providers of public goods, social services or other activities worth supporting. The second is to set eligibility conditions for the subsidy and check compliance with them.

The first way is analogous to the centrally planned economy with all its problems (inefficiency, information asymmetry, incentives for recipients to distort information, corruption climate, moral hazard).

The second way is the subject of many theoretical and empirical analyses, for example in the context of conditionality and fungibility.

Subsidy conditionality influences the recipient's behaviour in such a way as to make it comply with the ideas of the donor as far as possible. Sachs and Svensson have developed microeconomic models[134] in which conditionality improves the outcome from the donor's perspective when services are provided through an agency that does not entirely share the donor's preferences (in this case the government, which can implement reforms that improve the outcome from the subsidy provider's perspective; however, the effort to implement reforms enters its utility function with a negative sign). Ranaweera studies the relationship between conditionality and the necessary amount of aid on the basis of the Harrod-Domar macroeconomic model.[135] Ellerman discusses

---

133 This would be economically rational only in a deterministic decision-making situation. In such case it would indeed be optimal (economically rational) for the donor to provide the minimum amount needed to ensure the survival of a sufficient number of public goods providers. In reality, though, this boundary solution would mean, among other things, a high relative frequency of collapse of subsidized entities and a loss of confidence among recipients of public services. This is something that state decision-makers (politicians and civil servants) usually go to great lengths to avoid, as otherwise they would lose the political support of a large fraction of the electorate.

134 See Sachs, J.: Conditionality, Debt Relief, and the Developing Country Debt Crisis. In *Developing Country Debt and World Economy*, edited by J. Sachs, 275–84. Chicago: University of Chicago Press, 1989, or Svensson, J.: When Is Foreign Aid Policy Credible? Aid Dependence and Conditionality. *Journal of Development Economics* 61, 1(2000): 61–84.

135 See Ranaweera, T.: Foreign Aid, Conditionality and Ghost of the Financing Gap: A Forgotten Aspect of the Aid Debate. *World Bank Policy Research Paper* No. 3019, World Bank, 2003.

conditionality of aid in the light of various models based on social learning and change.[136] Killick discusses the potential costs of conditionality in the sense of reduced effectiveness of aid.[137] Cordella and Dellaricia construct a microeconomic optimization model for the case where the donor and the recipient have different criteria.[138]

Fungibility refers to the fact that a subsidized entity can avoid conditionality if it is funded from multiple uncoordinated sources. If, for example, a donor makes aid conditional on its being used for educational programmes rather than arms projects, the recipient may accept the subsidy but then reduce spending on education and increase arms expenditure by the same amount, thereby bypassing the conditionality.[139]

In the following text we draw attention to another risk limiting the rules for receiving aid. These rules can have such a limiting effect that they prevent the optimal allocation of resources, since they can imply, for example, the needless demise of too many social service providers or public goods producers. Their previously incurred costs and their tangible and intangible assets can also be rendered worthless.

Although a donor may have good reasons for making a subsidy conditional (influencing the behaviour of recipients, limiting the misuse of subsidies for the benefit of public goods and services providers, or complying with budget regulations), doing so can lead to lower spending efficiency. We will show this using two simple models based on generalized microeconomics in which economic agents maximize the Pareto probability of their economic survival. In the first model, we examine the consequences of the donor prohibiting the carry-over of unused subsidies to the next period. The second model analyses a rule limiting the overhead costs of a subsidized social services provider, motivated, for example, by a lack of trust or by concerns about the misuse of the subsidy at the expense of service recipients. We will show that such restrictions can be counterproductive from the donor's perspective, i.e. they can contradict the purpose of the subsidy.

In our models, we assume that the donor's criterion when deciding on the allocation of a subsidy is to achieve the maximum possible return on his money in favour of public or social service recipients.

---

136 See Ellerman, D.: Hirschmanian Themes of Social Learning and Change. *World Bank Policy Research Working Paper*, No. 2591, World Bank, 2001.

137 See Killick, T.: Principals, Agents, and the Failings of Conditionality. *Journal of Institutional Development* 9, 4(1997): 483–95.

138 See Cordella, T. – Dellaricia, G.: Limits of Conditionality in Poverty Reduction Programs. *IMF Staff Papers* 49(2002): 68–86.

139 This problem is studied at the theoretical level by, for example, Devarajan, S., Swaroop, V.: The Implications of Foreign Aid Fungibility for Development Assistance. *World Bank Policy Research Working Paper* No. 2022, World Bank, 1998. Empirical research has been conducted by, for example, Feyzioglu, T., Swarroop, V., Zhu, M.: A Panel Data Analysis of the Fungibility of Foreign Aid. *The World Bank Economic Review* 12, 1(1998): 29–58.

Let us start by assuming that the donor (state) has decided on the total amount of the subsidy granted to providers of a particular public service. Its objective function when seeking the optimal allocation of funds involves maximizing the volume of services provided[140] (obviously to an acceptable/prescribed standard, with the donor checking compliance with this condition).[141] An economically rational donor with such an objective function allocates its limited resources among the subsidy recipients in such a way as to ensure that as many as possible of them (of the prescribed standard) survive. Accordingly, it tries to ensure the highest possible probability of economic survival of the subsidized entities.

The donor (state) does not interfere in the recipient's routine decision-making, but sets conditions or rules for the ongoing provision of the subsidy.

Such conditions need not be limited to service quality. The donor does not have to (but can) allow the carry-over of unused portions of the subsidy to the next period, and can (but does not have to) prescribe allocation of the subsidy by purpose (for example it can prescribe a maximum permissible ratio for overhead or wage costs).

Here, however, we need to make a distinction. Although a specific recipient that provides a low-quality public service is disqualified from receiving a subsidy in accordance with the objective function of the economically rational donor, restrictive rules for receiving a subsidy can contradict the purpose of the subsidy—they can lead *ceteris paribus* to a lower volume of service provision. If a donor (for example a grant agency) announces such a rule, it is being economically irrational, as it is—with a high probability (bordering on certainty)—deliberately excluding its own optimum from the set of feasible solutions.

Just as in the rest of this book, we adopt a microeconomic approach to the analysis and description of economic phenomena. We focus on themes that pertain to the allocation of public funds, but we refrain from investigating the macroeconomic context and only assess the rationality of the rules for allocating public funds among individual subsidy recipients.

In the following section, we will show that a microeconomic model[142] constructed on the principles of generalized microeconomics can help to provide answers to questions concerning the rationality of allocation of public funds.

---

140 This problem is the reciprocal of the maximization of productivity subject to technical feasibility. This relationship is analogous to the reciprocal problems of maximizing profit and minimizing costs at a given level of output in the theory of the firm.

141 This subsidy strategy applies solely to decision-making on the allocation of the subsidy in question. Both state and private donors naturally also have their own broader criterion within which their subsidy strategy runs.

142 See Hlaváček, J., Hlaváček, M.: Ekonomická iracionalita donátora plynoucí z nedůvěry k příjemci dotace. *Finance a úvěr* 54, 3–4(2004): 138–54.

10.5 SOME DEBATABLE PRINCIPLES/RULES
OF THE DONOR ACTIVITIES OF THE STATE

In this section we present models that show how much the subsidy rules set by the donor (state) can constitute economically irrational exclusion of its optimum. We will analyse and discuss the following rules for receiving subsidies:

- the donor (state) prohibits carry-over of the subsidy from one budget period to another,
- the state prescribes a maximum ratio for the provider's overhead costs in relation to the subsidy provided.

Although there may be good reasons for such restrictions (e.g. compliance with budget regulations), we should point out that they are not without their costs. Again, there is a trade-off: the subsidy provider enforces its will (as expressed by the rules) at the cost of lower spending efficiency. Such restrictions can therefore be counterproductive, acting against the primary intentions of the donor. We are talking here about real phenomena, not just model-based speculation.

The ban on the carry-over of unused parts of the subsidy leads to waste at the end of the year. This is usually caused by unforeseen problems with drawing the subsidy, due, among other things, to the impossibility of precisely estimating needs and prices in advance and of perfectly meeting deadlines in the relatively distant future.

Moreover, strict rules limiting the free will of the recipient regarding the allocation of the subsidy among individual material items (overheads, wages, investment) in fact represents a threat of limited efficiency of the subsidy. There is again a trade-off: on the one hand the state (donor) enforces its will in the rules of use of the subsidy and tries to avoid the threat of misuse of the subsidy; on the other hand it "pays" for this in terms of reduced efficiency of the subsidy, as some public goods providers, for example, will go out of business, taking their knowledge and skills (acquired partly thanks to previous subsidies) with them. Limiting wage funds to a fraction of the total amount of a scientific grant, for instance, can cause a brain drain of young researchers, especially in scientific fields where human resources are the biggest bottleneck.

The decision of the donor (state) can therefore (economically irrationally) contain a contradiction between its behaviour and its criterion (the purpose of its donor activity).

The first of the following two models will allow us to evaluate the impact of an obligation to use up the funds provided in a given fiscal period. The second model quantifies the results of a ban on using public funds in a non-prescribed way.

In both models we assume that the donor financially supports the social public service provider with the aim of maximizing its probability of survival.

For simplicity, we also assume that the provider is wholly dependent on the contribution (subsidy, grant) provided by the donor (e.g. the state).

We assume that the subsidy provider endeavours in "Darwinian" fashion to maximize the Pareto probability of its own survival.[143] Agents that behave in contradiction to this criterion will simply not survive, and the ambition of the model is to describe the behaviour of economic survivors.

Suppose that the survival of subsidy recipients (social service providers) depends exclusively on their income and that the subsidy is their only revenue. Extinction (non-survival) of a recipient is given by its inability to perform the social service in question.

In this section we assume that the behaviour of an agent is determined not by the relative margin itself, but by the increase/decrease therein. This is consistent with the psychological Weber–Fechner law,[144] according to which individuals in many cases decide not according to the intensity of a stimulus, but according to the change in the intensity of the stimulus. This assumption is consistent with a second-order Pareto probability distribution, for which the risk of extinction decreases in proportion to the square of the distance from the extinction zone.[145] This is presented in more detail in section 1.3.2.

The reason why, unlike in previous chapters, we do not use the first-order Pareto distribution is that we are dealing here in fact with the criterion of a politician who always maximizes his probability of political survival in office and who knows from experience that voters put greater weight on the rate of growth of their standard of living than on the absolute level thereof.

10.5.1 RESULT OF NON-TRANSFERABILITY OF A SUBSIDY TO THE NEXT PERIOD—OPTIMAL SUBSIDY TIMING MODEL

Let us start by assuming that a subsidy recipient having the preferences described in the previous section can freely carry over any unused part of the subsidy to the next period and that the funding need in the two periods is the same. For simplicity, we will consider two consecutive periods with the same extinction boundary (subsistence level).

At the optimum of an economically rational donor, it must hold that the marginal transfer of funds from the first period to the second will reduce the recipient's probability of extinction in the first period to the same extent as it will increase its probability of extinction in the second period.

---

143 As we argued earlier (in the introduction and in section 5.1), all agents must implicitly respect this criterion in their decision-making, even if they have a different explicit (subjective) criterion.

144 For more on the Weber–Fechner law, see section 1.3.2.

145 Whereas for the first-order Pareto distribution the risk of extinction decreases in proportion to the distance from the extinction zone.

We will now derive the optimal subsidy timing. We use the following notation:

d the recipient's income,

b the recipient's subsistence level (extinction zone boundary),

a the total subsidy for the two consecutive periods from the donor (state),

a_t the subsidy from the donor (state) provided to the recipient in the t-th period.

As we justified at the end of the previous section, we assume that the risk of extinction of the recipient as perceived by the donor is determined not by the relative income margin vis-à-vis the subsistence level $r(d) = \dfrac{d-b}{d} = 1 - \dfrac{b}{d}$, but

by the change therein $r'(d)$. We therefore assume that the agent's survival corresponds to an asymmetric second-order Pareto probability distribution[146] with probability density function

$$f(d) = \frac{2b^2}{d^3} \qquad \text{for} \quad d \geq b,$$

$$f(d) = 0 \qquad \text{for} \quad d < b$$

and with distribution function

$$F(d) = \max\left[0;\ 1 - \left(\frac{b}{d}\right)^2\right].$$

We assume for simplicity that the subsidy is the sole income of the subsidy recipient (a public service provider), i.e. $d = a$.

We will set $b = 1$ (that is how we select the money unit). Suppose, furthermore, that the overall subsidy amount for the two periods a is fixed and that survival in both periods is not ruled out, i.e. that

$$a_1 + a_2 = a > 2.$$

By applying the second-order Pareto distribution we obtain:

$$p_t(a_t) = 0 \qquad \text{for} \quad a_t < 1,$$

$$= 1 - \left(\frac{1}{a_t}\right)^2 \qquad \text{for} \quad a_t \geq 1.$$

---

146 See section 1.3.2 for the properties of the second-order Pareto distribution.

Remember that the donor's criterion is maximization of the recipient's survival probability, which is given by the product of the (let us assume mutually independent) survival probabilities in the two periods:

$$p(a_1, a_2) = p_1(a_1) \cdot p_2(a_2) = \left[1 - \left(\frac{1}{a_1}\right)^2\right] \cdot \left[1 - \left(\frac{1}{a_2}\right)^2\right].$$

The donor solves the constrained optimization problem:

$$\max_{a_1 + a_2 \leq a} p(a_1, a_2),$$

which can be transformed into the free optimization problem:

$$\max L(a_1, a_2, \lambda) = \max \left[p(a_1, a_2) + \lambda(a - a_1 - a_2)\right] =$$

$$= \max \left[\left[1 - \left(\frac{1}{a_1}\right)^2\right] \cdot \left[1 - \left(\frac{1}{a_2}\right)^2\right] + \lambda(a - a_1 - a_2)\right].$$

Differentiating function $L(a_1, a_2, \lambda)$ with respect to all its three variables gives us the necessary conditions for the optimum:

$$a_1 \cdot (1 - a_1^2) = a_2 \cdot (1 - a_2^2),$$

$$a_1 + a_2 = a.$$

The optimal solution is therefore (not surprisingly) regular granting of the subsidy:

$$a_1 = a_2 = \frac{a}{2}.$$

The recipient's survival probability is given by the product of the (let us assume mutually independent[147]) survival probabilities in the two periods:

---

147 This is a simplifying assumption that abstracts from the fact that an increase in the subsidy in the first period can in reality cause the survival probability in the second period to either increase (owing to a smaller covered equipment maintenance debt) or to decrease (owing to higher maintenance costs of equipment purchased in the first period).

$$p(a_1,a_2) = p\left(\frac{a}{2},\frac{a}{2}\right) = \left[\frac{\frac{a}{2}-b}{\frac{a}{2}}\right]^2 = \left[1-\frac{2b}{a}\right]^2.$$

Let us now examine the implications of the fact that the time distribution of the subsidy does not correspond to the recipient's needs. In the case of uniform needs, such a mismatch represents irregularity in the provision of the subsidy. Let us denote the difference between the higher and lower subsidy by $\delta > 0$, that is:

$$a_1 = \frac{a+\delta}{2},$$

$$a_2 = \frac{a-\delta}{2}.$$

If the subsidy is well above the threat zone boundary ($d \gg b = 1$), a slight irregularity in the provision of the subsidy will have no effect. If, however, the subsidy is close to this boundary and the probability of survival is much less than unity, this irregularity can threaten the recipient, as its survival probability will be significantly reduced. The relative decrease as a result of an undesirable (i.e. not matching the recipient's needs) shift of a portion of the subsidy δ is:

$$\frac{\Delta p}{p} = \frac{p\left(\frac{a}{2},\frac{a}{2}\right) - p\left(\frac{a+\delta}{2},\frac{a-\delta}{2}\right)}{p\left(\frac{a}{2},\frac{a}{2}\right)}.$$

Figure 68 and Figure 69 show the effect of the relative deviation from subsidy regularity $\frac{\delta}{a}$ on the relative decrease in survival probability $\frac{\Delta p}{p}$ (both in %) for an agent with a threat equal to the mean of the Pareto distribution $b=\frac{a}{2}$ and for an agent with a threat equal to the median of the Pareto distribution $b=\frac{a}{\sqrt{2}}$.

Figure 68: The relation between the relative decrease in survival probability (in %) and the relative deviation from a regular subsidy (in %) for an agent with a threat equal to the mean of the second-order Pareto distribution

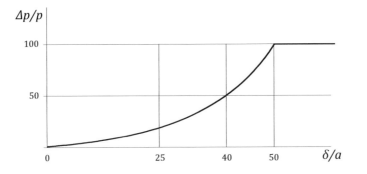

It is clear from Figure 68 that for an agent with an average subsidy (i.e. a subsidy equal to double the subsistence level) an irregularity whereby half the annual grant is moved to another period will be ruinous for the recipient. Shifting 40% of the annual grant will reduce its probability of survival by roughly one half.

Figure 69 concerns an agent which is, as far as the threat is concerned, at the midpoint of the series of all agents ranked according to threat level, i.e. an agent at the median $a = b \cdot \sqrt{2}$.

Figure 69: Ditto for an agent with a threat equal to the median of the second-order Pareto distribution $b = \dfrac{a}{\sqrt{2}}$

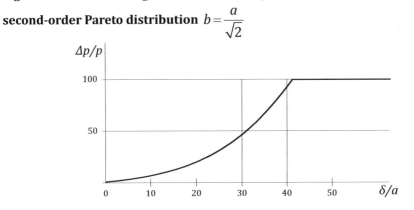

A subsidy fluctuation of 40% of the subsidy will fatally endanger the median agent and all economically weaker agents (by comparison with the median agent) and will also significantly threaten the other agents. A 30% deviation will mean *ceteris paribus* an almost 50% reduction in the survival probability of the median agent (and hence also of more than half of the agents).

We arrive at the same conclusions for the case where, conversely, the subsidy is regular (equal in both periods) but the needs change. This time profile can also imply a significant bottleneck for periods when needs are greater.

The donor is reliant on information from recipients and therefore does not have objective information about their needs in individual periods.

One option is to have a regular regime. In the case of different needs in different periods (possibly ascertained by the recipient only during the second period), this fundamentally reduces the agent's probability of survival, i.e. it runs counter to the point of the subsidy. Here again, we can describe the rate of decline in the agent's survival probability on a subsidy equal to double the subsistence level by means of the chart in Figure 68.

Another option is to have an irregular but pre-agreed subsidy. However, this presupposes that the recipient knows his needs in the coming years exactly and a long way in advance and that these needs will not change over time. An unexpected change in needs—which cannot be ruled out in reality—can then cause a reduction in the probability of survival and a decrease in the efficiency of the subsidy (as measured by the effect of the social or public services per money unit issued by the state).

The restriction on carrying over public budget funding from one period (year) to another is based on numerous factors and practical problems. The main causes (explicit or implicit) of this constraint are the following:

- the technology used to draw up public budgets,
- a lack of trust of the central authority in the honesty of recipients, including a lack of trust (justified or unjustified) in the objectivity of the information provided to it by the recipients,
- a lack of trust on the part of the recipient that his information openness will not backfire on him (leading to distortion of information),
- the efforts of the central authority to reduce the "moral hazard" whereby the recipients force the donor to provide funds de facto by blackmail and the recipients of the social or public service play the role of hostages of the subsidy recipients.

Whatever the cause of the restriction on carrying over funding from one period to another, it does constitute a specific type of money wasting. It is a *sui generis* case of the prisoner's dilemma, since the lack of trust here prevents efficient behaviour of the system and optimal efficiency of use of the funding provided by the donor (state).

In the following model we will analyse the consequences of a different type of lack of trust of the donor in the recipients. In this case, the donor prescribes the subsidy use structure in an attempt to prevent the subsidy from being misused, for example, for excessive (in the donor's judgment) personal enrichment or for excessive overhead or investment spending.

10.5.2 PRESCRIBED SUBSIDY USE STRUCTURE

In this model we will try to address the problem of the effect that the donor's lack of trust has when the process of granting social or public services is rather more structured than in the previous model. We will differentiate here between subsidy recipients and service recipients. Hence, we assume a model with three levels of agents on a hierarchical scale:

a) a donor (state) providing a subsidy for the provision of a social or public service (which it is unable to provide efficiently itself),

b) subsidy recipients providing a social or public service, who cease to exist if they are unable to do so,

c) recipients of the service.

We assume that there are multiple subsidy recipients providing the social or public service, so that the collapse of one subsidy recipient does not imply the collapse of the service.[148]

We also assume that each subsidy recipient behaves in such a way that both it and the recipients of its service survive jointly (do not collapse) with maximum probability.[149] In this sense, we depart from Svensson's microeconomic models of conditionality,[150] in which the objective functions of the donor and the recipient are different (the principal-agent approach).

We assume that the partial probabilities of economic extinction of the service provider and recipient are independent and that the collapse of all service recipients would mean the collapse of the subsidy recipient as well, since a fatal failure in the provision of the service would disqualify the subsidy recipient in the eyes of the donor (an assumption of independence of the partial probabilities of extinction and of existential dependence of the subsidy recipient on the service recipient).

Economic extinction of the subsidy recipient (and simultaneously the service provider) can be caused by:

- a real impossibility of providing the service at the given revenue level,
- excessively low income of the subsidy recipient, forcing it to change its line of business,
- collapse of the service recipient.

---

148 This assumption allows us to abstract from the moral hazard effect in the model.

149 This does not necessarily mean that maximization of the probability of survival is an explicit criteria of public service recipients. Their criterion is some sort of subjective utility. However, the survival of a public service recipient is part of the decision-making problem of the public service provider. For the latter it is crucial that the former does not collapse, because such collapse could cause its own economic extinction.

150 Svensson, J.: When Is Foreign Aid Policy Credible? Aid Dependence and Conditionality. *Journal of Development Economics* 61, 1(2000): 61–84.

The subsidy recipient will seek the optimum allocation of the subsidy between its own overheads (including subsistence) and its service recipients. A distrustful donor (state) will intervene to change this optimum. Suppose it orders the subsidy recipient to reduce its overhead spending by $\delta\%$ in favour of the service recipients. In so doing it may increase the probability of the subsidy recipient walking out like an "unhappy wife", i.e. it may unwittingly create a bottleneck for the subsidy recipient which will increase its probability of collapse (extinction) in the sense of an inability to provide the given social or public service.[151] We will quantify this causality in the following model.

As we justified above, we assume a second-order Pareto distribution for the survival (non-failure) of agents. We use this probability distribution both for subsidy recipients and for service recipients.

We use the following notation in the model:

a the amount of the subsidy,

d the subsidy recipient's income which is used directly by the service recipient (i.e. the value of the services provided to it),

r the overhead costs of the subsidy recipient,

b_d the subsistence level (extinction zone boundary) of the subsidy recipient,

b_s ditto for the service recipient,

p_d the probability of survival of the subsidy recipient,

p_s ditto for the service recipient.

As in the previous model we assume a second-order Pareto probability distribution for the subjective probability of survival of the two agents (the subsidy recipient and the service recipient):

$$p_d(r) = 0 \qquad \text{for} \quad r < b_d,$$

$$= 1 - \left(\frac{b_d}{r}\right)^2 \qquad \text{for} \quad r \geq b_d,$$

$$p_s(d) = 0 \qquad \text{for} \quad d < b_s,$$

$$= 1 - \left(\frac{b_s}{d}\right)^2 \qquad \text{for} \quad d \geq b_s.$$

For clarity we abstract from the problem of mandatory timing of expenditures used in the previous model. This corresponds to an assumption that the state

---

151 A major Czech grant agency provides research grants with the proviso that no more than 10% of the grant is spent on wages and salaries, yet the wages of young researchers and teachers are undoubtedly a bottleneck for fundamental research work in the Czech Republic.

leaves the time distribution of the subsidy into individual phases entirely to the subsidy recipient. In this sense, therefore, the state trusts the subsidy recipient. The lack of trust studied in this model is of a different kind: the state tries to prevent the subsidy recipient from enriching itself at the expense of the service recipients.

This can be a good thing (in areas dominated by fiercely competitive agents trying to make the maximum short-term profit), but it can also be a bad thing (in areas dominated by altruistic, long-term providers of social or public services). In our model, we will focus on the second type of subsidy recipients providing public or social services.[152]

Given the above assumptions (including the assumption of independence of the partial probabilities of extinction and of existential dependence of the subsidy recipient on the service recipient; see above), the probability of non-failure of a social service provider is given by the product of the probabilities of (economic) survival of the subsidy recipient and the service recipients:

$$p(r,d) = p_d(r) \cdot p_s(d).$$

A rational subsidy recipient decides to divide amount a between its overheads r and its costs for providing services to the service recipient d in the way described by the following constrained optimization problem:

$$\max_{r+d \le a} p(r,d).$$

A subsidy recipient maximizing (explicitly or implicitly) its own probability of survival solves the problem of optimal allocation of the subsidy between its overheads and the service recipient in a manner corresponding to the solution of the problem:

$$\max_{r+d \le a} p(r,d) = \max_{r+d \le a}\left(1 - \left(\frac{b_d}{r}\right)^2\right)\cdot\left(1 - \left(\frac{b_s}{d}\right)^2\right).$$

We can transform this constrained optimization problem into a free optimization problem using the Lagrange function:

$$\max L(r,d,\lambda) = \max\left[\left(1 - \left(\frac{b_d}{r}\right)^2\right)\cdot\left(1 - \left(\frac{b_s}{d}\right)^2\right) + \lambda \cdot (a - r - d)\right].$$

---

152 In the future we would like to dynamize the model and investigate how the approach (allocation rule) of the donor determines the type of climate.

We obtain the necessary conditions for the optimum by setting the partial derivatives of function L with respect to all its three variables r, d and λ equal to zero. In this way we derive a system of three equations:

$$\left[1-\left(\frac{b_s}{d}\right)^2\right]\cdot\frac{b_d^{\,2}}{r^3}+2\lambda=0\,,$$

$$\left[1-\left(\frac{b_d}{r}\right)^2\right]\cdot\frac{b_s^{\,2}}{d^3}+2\lambda=0\,,$$

$$r+d=a.$$

From the first two equations we get:

$$\left[1-\left(\frac{b_s}{d}\right)^2\right]\cdot\frac{b_d^{\,2}}{r^3}=\left[1-\left(\frac{b_d}{r}\right)^2\right]\cdot\frac{b_s^{\,2}}{d^3}\,. \qquad (*)$$

If the threat to the subsidy recipient happens to be equal to the threat to the recipients of its service, the solution is $r^* = d^* = \dfrac{a}{2}$, i.e. it is optimal for the subsidy recipient to spend half of the money provided by the donor on its overheads. If the threats are unequal (i.e. if $b_d \neq b_s$), it is optimal to favour the more threatened agent.

As in the model in the previous section, we will focus on a service provider with mean income, i.e. (for the second-order Pareto distribution) with a subsistence level that is half the income level. Assuming that:

$$b_d + b_s = 2$$

(that is how we select the money unit),

$$a = 2\cdot(b_d + b_s) = 4\,.$$

After substituting into equation (*) we obtain:

$$\left(r^2 - b_d^{\,2}\right)\cdot\left(2-b_d\right)^2\cdot r^2 - \left(4-r\right)^2\cdot\left[\left(4-r\right)^2 - \left(2-b_d\right)^2\right]\cdot b_d^{\,2} = 0\,.$$

The following figure shows the relationship between the solution to this equation (with unknown r and parameter b_d) and the parameter.[153] For $b_d = b_s = 1$ (equal threats to the subsidy recipient and the service recipient) the solution is $r^* = 2$ (half of the subsidy $a = 4$ will go on overheads). For $b_d \to 0_+$ and $b_s \to 0_+$ the whole subsidy goes to the more threatened agent (i.e. $r^* \to 0_+$ and $r^* \to 4_+$ respectively). If $b_d > b_s$, i.e. if the subsidy recipient is the more threatened, it will choose overhead costs exceeding half of the total subsidy. If, however, $b_d < b_s$, i.e. if the service recipient is the more threatened, the subsidy recipient will reduce its overhead costs in its own interests to below half of the subsidy, to the extent illustrated in Figure 70.

Figure 70: The optimal overhead level (from the subsidy recipient's point of view) for an agent with a threat equal to the mean of the second-order Pareto distribution

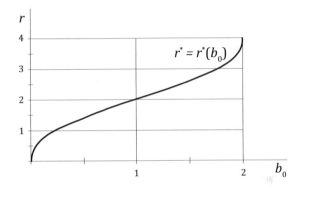

It can be seen from Figure 70 that when the general threat level is high, the preference for the more threatened agent is greater.

The most important conclusion is that a subsidy recipient acting in its own interests does not maximize its overheads. On the contrary, in certain situations it will reduce them, despite not being forced to do so. If, however, it is forced to reduce them against its will, both the subsidy recipient and the service recipient may collapse.

We will now quantify this risk for three illustrative cases:
- equal threats to both ($b_d = b_s = 1$),
- service recipient more threatened ($b_d = 0.5$, $b_s = 1$),
- subsidy recipient more threatened ($b_d = 1.5 = 2b_s$).

---

153 We solved the equation numerically. For all parameters $b_0 \in \langle 0, 2 \rangle$ in the interval $\langle 0, 4 \rangle$ the equation has a unique solution. The other solutions are nonsensical.

In the case of equal threats to both agents, the survival probability attains its maximum possible values for $r = 2$. How much does the survival probability decrease if the donor puts a cap on overhead spending?

Figure 71: The reduction in the subsidy recipient's survival probability for sub-optimal overheads (100% corresponds to the maximum survival probability for the individual cases)

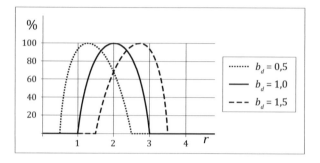

It can be seen from Figure 71 that in the case of equal threats to the subsidy recipient and the service recipient ($b_d = b_s = 1$), a cap on overhead costs of less than or equal to 25% of the total subsidy will cause the certain demise of the subsidy recipient. Even for the case where the service recipient is more threatened ($b_d = 0.5$ and $b_s = 1$), when the maximum survival probability occurs when overheads $r = 1.25$ (i.e. 31% of the total subsidy), a 25% cap on overhead costs means a reduction in its probability of survival. A donor-imposed cap of one-eighth of the total subsidy will certainly ruin the subsidy recipient. Such a danger applies most of all, of course, in the case where the subsidy recipient is more threatened ($b_d = 1.5 = 2b_s$), where a cap on overhead spending of one-third of the total subsidy is enough to lead to certain extinction.

In the interests of its own survival, a rational subsidy recipient will not "rip off" service recipients, as by doing so it would be cutting its own throat (if, as we assume, it wishes to survive in the role of service provider). If the donor (state) trusts it, everything is okay. If, however, the donor (in an effort to ensure that service recipients get a greater share) constrains the subsidy recipient by setting a cap on overhead costs as a proportion of the total subsidy, there are two possibilities: the cap—motivated by the donor's lack of trust—is either of no significance (the subsidy recipient would satisfy it of his own free will anyway), or represents a reduction in survival probability. Such a cap can even be a lethal weapon—in all the cases described above a condition that the subsidy recipient's own consumption should not exceed one-tenth of the subsidy (see footnote 151) would itself preclude the economic survival of practically every subsidy recipient.

Wherever possible, a rational donor (state) provides subsidies with trust in the recipient's reliability, since limiting rules can fundamentally reduce the efficiency of use of the subsidy, even though their original and sole purpose was the exact opposite.

We are not trying to saying that it is possible or necessary to remove all state-imposed constraints on the use of public money. If there is a low level of competition, or if subsidized public service providers have insufficiently long histories, the threat of misuse of the subsidy is greater and the donor's rules to prevent such misuse should be stricter. The same applies in reverse—gradually earned trust in a subsidy recipient allows a rational donor to increase the efficiency of the subsidy by relaxing the rules of use of the subsidy for "tried and tested" recipients.

We merely wish to point out that the standard economic trade-off applies to subsidies. The donor (state) pays for control of the use of such funding with a reduction in the efficiency of service provision. It is a prisoner's dilemma of sorts—a lack of trust between agents (in our case the donor's unwillingness to believe that the recipient will not misuse the subsidy by time-shifting part of it or by charging high overhead costs) can be a cause of economically irrational behaviour.

In this sense, too, a lack of trust can be expensive and trust can be economically rational.

CONCLUSION

To conclude this book we will summarise the most important findings offered by the generalization of standard microeconomics, which replaces the profit criterion with the more general maximization of the Pareto probability of economic survival.

The scope of the issues that can be modelled thanks to such generalization is in our view remarkable. We have been moving in areas that are beyond the range of standard microeconomics based on the *homo economicus* paradigm: the behaviour of a firm in a centrally planned economy with an anti-efficient economic climate; an economy with widespread corporate insolvency; the optimum in a sector showing increasing returns to scale; the market allocation of externalities; the economic behaviour of agents in the non-profit university sector; and altruism and rational redistribution from the microeconomic perspective. In addition, generalization of the criterion function gives us a non-standard and deeper perspective on certain problems that are dealt with by standard microeconomics, such as risk modelling and risk aversion and the principal–agent problem (moral hazard and adverse selection)

In *Chapter 1* we formulated the general microeconomic criterion in terms of maximization of the probability of survival. We noted that the assumption that the probability of survival is directly proportional to the margin relative to the subsistence level (i.e. the boundary of the zone of certain extinction) is consistent with a first-order Pareto probability distribution. In this way we solved the problem of construction of the cardinal utility function for non-profit agents and for agents that have other criteria besides the profit criterion.

Chapter 2, dealing with risk modelling and hedging against risk, offered a non-traditional look at the traditional St. Petersburg paradox. The results generated by the model are intuitively more acceptable than both the 250-year-old explanation of this paradox by Daniel Bernoulli and the more than 50-year-old explanation of von Neumann. In our opinion these explanations had not previously been surpassed. The generalized economics approach also inspired us to introduce a new category of "situational risk attraction"—agents can be forced by their situation to take risks (even if they are risk averse "by nature") because only by doing so do they have at least a non-zero probability of avoiding otherwise inevitable economic extinction.

The generalization of economic agents' criterion to maximization of the probability of survival subject to certain conditions guarantees the existence of market equilibrium even in cases where standard microeconomics with agents maximizing the utility of expected income rules out such equilibrium. This we proved in *Chapter 3*. Generalization of the profit criterion allowed us to model decision-making with two criteria (the utility of a principal and the utility of an agent). This is particularly useful in the case where certain entities knowingly affect the prosperity of other entities or where the economic extinction of one entity can threaten the survival of other entities. We arrived at the conclusion that given the assumption of maximization of the probability of survival, the problems associated with information asymmetry in principal–agent models are weaker than in a standard economic climate of entities maximizing their expected profit, because the principal and the agent are not in a fully antagonistic relationship. If the survival of the agent is contingent on the survival of the principal, the problem of adverse selection disappears. The problem of moral hazard also decreases: under certain (not unrealistic) conditions, an agent will voluntarily spend to reduce his level of risk. We consider it proven that generalized microeconomics offers a more realistic view than "anonymous" profit maximization for many principal–agent problems.

The methodological approach of generalized microeconomic theory also proved very successful in insurance decision-making models, as dealt with in *Chapter 4*. Maximization of the probability of survival allowed us to model the fact that the agent's economic situation is the key factor for his insurance decision (and consequently for his insurance demand function). Agents with extremely high income will reject insurance (as an unfair game). However, agents with extremely low income will not buy insurance either, because if they did they would have to forgo other, more necessary consumer goods. The existing standard models with maximization of expected utility (von Neumann) and the best-known non-standard model (Kahneman–Tversky) capture this tendency which occurs in the real economy either not at all or only partially.

Chapter 5 examines economic rationality in the non-profit sector using the example of universities. Here we summarize the results of an analysis of the consequences of various university funding modalities. We assume that every university at every stage maximizes its probability of survival, which is threatened by low income and loss of accreditation due to teachers quitting for better paid jobs. The control variables are the tuition fee and teachers' pay. An excessively high tuition fee deters students, whereas an unnecessarily low tuition fee represents an opportunity cost, thereby worsening the university's economic position. Likewise, unnecessarily high lecturers' pay endangers the university's financial situation, while excessively low pay increases the likelihood of lecturers quitting and the likelihood of loss of accreditation. In simulation experiments, we compared the impacts of various funding modalities (tuition fees only, a combination of tuition fees and subsidies, and no tuition fees, i.e. state subsidies only) on the behaviour and existential threat of the university and on the overall efficiency of the system (the number of study applicants satisfied, demand for teachers, the tuition fee and teachers' pay). In the final section of the chapter we derived the shape of the supply function for a university maximizing its probability of survival, i.e. the relation between the number of students and marginal revenue.

In *Chapter 6* we present the *homo se assecurans* model, the first version of which was constructed by the co-author of this book in the late 1980s. The producer's criterion there was maximization of the (absolute) reserve against the plan constraint. In our book we modify this model in such a way that the producer maximizes the relative reserve, in line with the other chapters. Both versions of the *homo se assecurans* model (in contrast to standard microeconomics) allow us to describe the situation where an economic agent prefers a production situation lying inside the production set (i.e. below the technological maximum). This situation was typical of centrally planned economies. The model lends support to the hypothesis of the unreformability of central planned economies in the sense of increasing their efficiency—even measures that would boost efficiency in a standard economic environment (such as "accommodative planning") lead inevitably to a further reduction in the efficiency of the economy in the *homo se assecurans* environment. Nonetheless, the model shows that the behaviour of agents in centrally planned economies was rational, even though this pathological rationality was caused by the very nature of the communist economic system, where economic survival (company managers remaining in their posts) necessitates a completely different type of behaviour. Even this type of behaviour, however, can be modelled by generalized microeconomics, and the model offers deeper insight into the patterns of behaviour of economic agents and the economy as a whole.

The fact that an economically non-standard environment does not rule out rational economic decision-making of a kind is confirmed by *Chapter 7*. There we present a model of an economy with widespread corporate insolvency in which firms sell part of their output to "non-payers" at a higher price (thereby boosting their book profit and increasing their chances of getting a bank loan) and part of it to "payers" at a lower price (thereby acquiring funds for wages and other immediate payments). The model shows what a company (implicitly) seeking to maximize its probability of survival will do with its output and what its (economically rational) decision on how to split its output between payers and non-payers depends on.

Generalized microeconomics also allows us to model non-standard phenomena in the production sector of a standard market economy, as shown in *Chapter 8*. Specific conditions in certain monopolistic or oligopolistic industries lead to a non-standard non-decreasing production function. This is phenomenon about which standard microeconomics can say nothing other than that the optimal scale of production tends to infinity. In reality, however, there are risks associated with the potential entry of a new competitor, which will force, say, a monopolistic producer to choose a compromise between higher profitability (which would allow a new competitor to pay the high entry costs) and a lower risk of losing its privileged market position.

Chapter 9 is devoted to models of market allocation of externalities, namely a model of the emissions permit market and a model allowing parties to negotiate compensation for a negative externality (the Coase theorem). Generalization of the Coase theorem for the case of agents maximizing their probability of economic survival revealed that both agents (the polluter and the injured party) will be better off under bargaining (the same as in the standard Coase theorem), but the amount of investment in environmental cleanup is not independent of the legal regime (unlike in the standard Coase theorem). We also examined the problem of the efficiency of acquiring and transferring information between agents bound by externalities where the survival of the information provider depends on the survival of another agent. A noteworthy and relatively surprising conclusion is that the acquisition and transfer of information is advantageous for both agents even when the information effect is smaller than the information acquisition and transfer cost. Even more remarkable is the fact that an increase in the information effect can paradoxically increase the size of the information (and thus also financial) support provided by the recipient of the externality.

In the final chapter, *Chapter 10*, we investigated the issues of redistribution and altruism. Even altruistic behaviour can be explained by maximization of the probability of survival, which is usually increased by a higher degree of redistribution. Achievement of the purpose of redistribution depends on the circumstances. Optimal redistribution depends not only on the decision-taker's criterion, but also on the amount of the shared resources. Situations arise where a marginal change in the key variable leads to a fundamental change in the optimal redistribution strategy. Despite the relatively complicated context, the generalized microeconomics approach allowed us to model this issue. For the criterion of a state donor we applied the second-order Pareto distribution, because the criterion of a politician is maximization of his probability of re-election, and that is decided by the rate of growth rather than the absolute level of the standard of living. We demonstrated how the setting of strict conditions for the use of a subsidy by the state reduces the efficiency of the subsidy.

The model of a profit-maximizing producer (the *homo economicus* paradigm) is a special case of the more general criterion of maximization of the Pareto probability of survival. Our approach, therefore, is a generalization of, not an alternative to, standard microeconomics. We feel it is a useful generalization, because it allows us for the first time to model decision-making in non-standard situations and to capture economic rationality in non-profit sectors of the economy.

REFERENCES

ADLER, M. D., POSNER, E. A., EDS.: *Cost-Benefit Analysis: Legal, Economic, and Philosophical Perspectives.* Chicago: University of Chicago Press, 2001.

AKERLOF, G. A.: Procrastination and Obedience. *American Economic Review* 81, 2 (1991): 1–19.

APPLEBAUM, E., KATZ, E.: Measures of Risk Aversion and Comparative Statics of Industry Equilibrium. *American Economic Review* 76, 3 (1986): 524–29.

ARROW, K. J. ET AL., EDS.: *Barriers to Conflict Resolution.* New York: Norton, 1995.

AXELROD, G.: *The Evolution of Cooperation.* New York: Basic Books, 1981.

BECKER, G. S.: The Theory of Social Interactions. *Journal of Political Economy* 82, 6 (1974): 1063–93.

BECKER, G. S.: Altruism, Egoism and Genetic Fitness: Economics and Sociobiology. *Journal of Economic Literature* 14, 3 (1976): 817–26.

BERNOULLI, D.: Specimen theoriae novae de mensura sortis. *Comentarii Academiae Scientiarum Imperialis Petropolitanae* 5 (1738): 175–92. English translation by L. Sommer in *Econometrica* 22, 1 (1954): 23–36.

BOLTON, P., DEWATRIPONT, M.: *Contact Theory.* Cambridge, MA: MIT Press, 2005.

BORTEL, L.: Ekonomická analýza práva: případ kontraktu a jednatelství [Economic Analysis of Law: Case of Contract and Agency]. *Politická ekonomie* 52, 1 (2004): 107–18

BRIXIOVÁ, Z., BULÍŘ, A.: Output Performance Under Central Planning: A Model of Poor Incentives. *Economic Systems* 27, 1 (2003): 27–39.

BUCHANAN, J. M.: An Economic Theory of Clubs. *Economica* 32, 125 (1965): 1–14.

BUCHANAN, J. M., YOON, Y. J.: Symmetric Tragedies: Commons and Anticommons. *Journal of Law and Economics* 43, 1 (2000): 1–14.

BULÍŘ, A.: Platební neschopnost: problém „reálné" nebo „peněžní" ekonomiky? [Financial Insolvency: Problem of "Real" or "Monetary" Economy?]. *Politická ekonomie* 42, 2 (1994): 155–70.

CAHLÍK, T. ET AL.: *Multiagentní přístupy v ekonomii* [Multiagent Approaches in Economics]. Praha: Karolinum, 2006.

CAHLÍK, T., HLAVÁČEK, J., MARKOVÁ, J.: Školné či dotace? (Simulace s modely systému vysokých škol) [Simulation with Models of Universities System: Schoolfee or Dotation?]. *Politická ekonomie* 56, 1 (2008): 54–66.

COASE, R. H.: The Problem of Social Cost. *Journal of Law and Economics* 3, Oct. (1960): 1–44.

COOK, K. S., ED.: *Trust in Society*. New York: Russell Sage Foundation, 2001.

CORDELLA, T., DELL'ARICIA, G.: Limits of Conditionality in Poverty Reduction Programs. *IMF Staff Papers* 49 (2002): 68–86.

DAŇHEL, J.: K problému asymetrie informací v pojišťovnictví [To the Problem of Asymmetry of Information in the System of Insurance]. *Politická ekonomie* 50, 6 (2002): 809–13.

DENIS, D. K., MCCONNELL, J. J.: International Corporate Governance. *Journal of Financial and Quantitative Analysis* 38, 1 (2003): 1–36.

DEVARAJAN, S., SWAROOP, V.: The Implications of Foreign Aid Fungibility for Development Assistance. *World Bank Policy Research Working Paper* No. 2022, World Bank, 1998.

DIAMOND, P., STIGLITZ, J. E.: Increases in Risk and Risk Aversion. *Journal of Economic Theory* 8, 3 (1974): 337–60.

DVOŘÁK, J.: Platit faktury včas se moc nenosí [To Pay Payable Accounts in time is not in Fashion]. http://www.mesec.cz/clanky/platit-faktury-vcas-se-moc-nenosi/ [15-02-2009 08:11 UTC].

EDWARDS, W.: The Theory of Decision Making. *Psychological Bulletin* 51, 4 (1954): 380–417.

ELLERMAN, D.: Hirschmanian Themes of Social Learning and Change. *World Bank Policy Research Working Paper* No. 2591, World Bank, 2001.

EPSTEIN, G. A., GINTIS, H. M., EDS.: *Macroeconomic Policy After the Conservative Era. Studies in Investment, Saving and Finance*. Cambridge: Cambridge University Press, 1995.

ETZIONI, A.: *The Moral Dimension. Toward a New Economics*. New York: The Free Press, 1988

FEYZIOGLU, T., SWARROOP, V., ZHU, M.: A Panel Data Analysis of the Fungibility of Foreign Aid. *The World Bank Economic Review* 12, 1 (1998): 29–58.

FRAIT, J.: Morální hazard a výstup z bankovního sektoru [Moral Hazard and Exit from Banking Sector]. *Finance a úvěr* 52, 3 (2002): 102–4.

FRANK, R. H.: *Microeconomics and Behavior*. 6th ed. New York: McGraw-Hill, 2006.

FRIEDMAN, M.: Windfalls, the "Horizon" and Related Concepts in the Permanent Income Hypothesis. In *Measurement in Economics*, C. F. Christ et al., 3–28. Stanford: Stanford University Press, 1963.

FROHLICH, N., HUNT, T., OPPENHEIMER, J., WAGNER, R. H.: Individual Contributions for Collective Goods: Alternative Models. *The Journal of Conflict Resolution* 19, 2 (1975): 310–29.

FUKUYAMA, R.: *Trust: The Social Virtues and the Creation of Prosperity*. London: Hamish Hamilton, 1995.

FURUBOTN, E. G., RICHTER, R.: *Institutions and Economic Theory. The Contribution of the New Institutional Economics*. Ann Arbor: University of Michigan Press, 1997.

GINTIS, H.: *Game Theory Evolving: A Problem-Centered Introduction to Modeling Strategic Interaction*. Princeton: Princeton University Press, 2000.

GRAVELLE, H., REES, R.: *Microeconomics*. 2nd ed. London: Longman, 1992.

HART, J. A., COWHEY, P. F.: Theories of Collective Goods Reexamined. *The Western Political Quarterly* 30, 3 (1977): 351–62.

HAYEK, F. A. VON: *The Road to Serfdom*. Chicago: University of Chicago Press, 2007.

HELLER, M. A.: The Tragedy of the Anticommons. Property in the Transition from Marx to Markets. *Harvard Law Review* 111, 3 (1998): 621–88.

HIRSCHMAN, A. O.: *Exit, Voice and Loyalty. Responses to Decline in Firms, Organizations, and States*. Cambridge, MA: Harvard University Press, 1970.

HLAVÁČEK, J.: Homo se assecurans. *Politická ekonomie* 35, 6 (1987): 633–39.

HLAVÁČEK, J.: K ekonomické subjektivitě plánovacího centra [To an Economic Subjectivity of the Planning Centre]. *Politická ekonomie* 36, 4 (1988): 1039–52.

HLAVÁČEK, J.: *Objektivizace informací v plánovacím dialogu – možnosti a meze* [Getting True for Information in Planning Dialogue – Possibilities and Limits]. Praha: Academia, 1989.

HLAVÁČEK, J.: Producers' Criteria in a Centrally Planned Economy. In *Optimal Decisions in Markets and Planned Economies*, edited by R. E. Quandt and D. Tříska, 41–52. Boulder, CO: Westview Press, 1990.

HLAVÁČEK, J.: Zobecněný princip chování firmy v tržní ekonomice. [Generalized Principle of Firm Behavior in Market Economy]. *Politická ekonomie* 48, 4 (2000): 515–28.

HLAVÁČEK, J.: Dynamický model soustavy univerzit [Dynamic Model of a System of Universities]. *WP IES* No. 90. Praha: Fakulta sociálních věd UK, 2005.

HLAVÁČEK, J. ET AL.: *Mikroekonomie sounáležitosti se společenstvím* [Microeconomics of Coexistence and Belonging to Partnership]. Praha: Karolinum, 1999.

HLAVÁČEK, J., HLAVÁČEK, M.: Optimum výrobce při stále rostoucích výnosech z rozsahu [Producer's Optimum Under Unremitting Increase of Returns to Scale]. *Politická ekonomie* 50, 5 (2002): 689–98.

HLAVÁČEK, J., HLAVÁČEK, M.: Petrohradský paradox a kardinální funkce užitku [St Petersburg Paradox and Cardinal Utility Function]. *Politická ekonomie* 52, 1 (2004): 48–60.

HLAVÁČEK, J., HLAVÁČEK, M.: Ekonomická iracionalita donátora plynoucí z nedůvěry k příjemci dotace [Economic Irrationality of the Donator Arising from his Low Confidence in Donation Recipient]. *Finance a úvěr* 54, 3–4 (2004): 138–54.

HLAVÁČEK, J., HLAVÁČEK, M.: Cruel Altruism. *Prague Economic Papers* 14, 4 (2005): 363–71.

HLAVÁČEK, J., HLAVÁČEK, M.: "Principal-Agent" Problem in the Context of the Economic Survival. *Acta Economica Pragensia* 14, 3 (2006): 18–33.

HLAVÁČEK, J., HLAVÁČEK, M.: Poptávková funkce na trhu s pojištěním: porovnání maximalizace paretovské pravděpodobnosti přežití s teorií EUT von Neumanna a Morgensterna a s prospektovou teorií Kahnemana a Tverského [Demand function on the insurance market: comparison of maximization of survival Pareto-probability with EUT theory (von-Neumann, Morgenstern) and with the Prospect theory (Kahneman, Tverski)]. *Czech Economic Review, Acta Universitatis Carolinae Oeconomica* 1, 2 (2007): 116–34.

HLAVÁČEK, J., KYSILKA, P., ZIELENIEC, J.: Plánování a averze k měření [Directive Planning and Aversion to Get Information]. *Politická ekonomie* 36, 5 (1988): 593–606.

HLAVÁČEK J., TŘÍSKA D.: Funkce plánového zadání a její vlastnosti [Funtction of Plan Setting and its Properties]. *Politická ekonomie* 35, 4 (1987): 389–99.

HLAVÁČEK, J., TŘÍSKA, D.: Planning authority and Its Marginal Rate of Substitution. *Ekonomicko-matematický obzor* 23, 1 (1987): 38–53.

HLAVÁČEK, J., TŘÍSKA, D.: *Úvod do mikroekonomické analýzy* [Introduction to Microeconomic Analysis]. Praha: Fakulta sociálních věd UK, 1991.

HLAVÁČEK, J., TŮMA, Z.: Bankruptcy in the Czech Economy. In *Bankruptcy and the Post-Communist Economies of East Central Europe*, K. Mizsei. New York: Institute for East-West Studies, 1993.

HLAVÁČEK, J., ZIELENIEC, J.: Trh práce v ekonomice, přecházející od plánu k trhu – teoretická východiska [Labor market in an economy in transition from plan to market]. *VP* No. 379. Praha: Ekonomický ústav ČSAV, 1991.

HLAVÁČEK, M.: Modely difuze technologií [Models of Technology Diffusion]. *WP IES* No. 1, Praha: Fakulta sociálních věd UK, 2001.

HLAVÁČEK, M.: Efektivnost pořízení a předávání informace mezi privátními subjekty s pozitivně-externalitní vazbou [Efficiency of Information Acquisition and Transfer Among Agents Connected by Positive-Externality Connection]. *WP IES* No. 32. Praha: Fakulta sociálních věd UK, 2003

HOLMSTROM, B.: Moral Hazard and Observability. *Bell Journal of Economics* 10, 1 (1979): 74–91.

HUNTER, H.: Optimal Tautness in Development Planning. *Economic Development and Cultural Change* 9, 4 (1961): 561–72.

JANDA, K.: Credit Guarantees in a Credit Market with Adverse Selection. *Prague Economic Papers* 12, 4 (2003): 331–49.

JANDA, K.: The comparison of credit subsidies and guarantees in transition and post-transition economies. *Ekonomický časopis* 53, 4 (2005): 383–98.

JANDA, K.: Agency Theory Approach to the Contracting between lender and Borrower. *Acta Oeconomica Pragensia* 14, 3 (2006): 34–47.

JENSEN, M. C., MECKLING, W. H.: Theory of the Firm: Managerial Behavior, Agency Costs and Ownership Structure. *Journal of Financial Economics* 3, 4 (1976): 305–60.

KAHNEMAN, D., TVERSKY, A.: Rational Choice and the Framing of Decisions. *Journal of Business* 59, 4 (1986): 251–78.

KEREN, M.: On the Tautness of Plans. *Review of Economic Studies* 39, 4 (1972): 469–86.

KILLICK, T.: Principals, Agents and the Failings of Conditionality. *Journal of International Development* 9, 4 (1997): 483–95.

KLUSOŇ, V.: *Instituce a odpovědnost. K filosofii ekonomické vědy* [To philosophy of economic science]. Praha: Karolinum, 2004.

KORNAI, J.: *Economics of Shortage*. Amsterdam: North Holland, 1980.

KOTULAN, A.: Konstrukce stimulační funkce indukující nezkreslené informace [Construction of stimulation function inducing unbiased information]. *Politická ekonomie* 32, 2 (1984): 250–65.

LAFFONT, J. J.: *Incentives and Political Economy*. Oxford: Oxford University Press, 2000.

MCMILLAN, J., ROTHSCHILD, M.: Searching for the Lowest Price when the Distribution of Prices is Unknown. *Journal of Political Economy* 82, 4 (1974): 689–711.

MAŇAS, M.: *Teorie her a optimální rozhodování* [Game Theory and Optimal Decision-making]. Praha: Státní pedagogické nakladatelství, 1969.

MASLOW, A. H.: *Motivation and Personality*. 2nd ed. New York: Harper and Row, 1970.

MEJSTŘÍK, M.: Corporate Governance, Ownership Concentration and FDI in CR. In *Corporate Re-structuring and Governance in Transition Economies*, edited by B. Dallago and I. Iwasaki, 65–90. London: Palgrave Macmillan, 2007.

MERTLÍK, P.: Česku hrozí druhotná platební neschopnost firem [Impendency of secondary insolvency of firms in the Czech Republic]. http://www.radio.cz/cz/clanek/111897 [08-01-2009 07:00 UTC].

MEYER, J.: Two-Moment Decision Models and Expected Utility Maximization. *American Economic Review* 77, 3 (1987): 421–30.

MILGRAM, S.: The Experience of Living in Cities. *Science* 167, 3924 (1970): 1461–68.

MIRRLEES, J. A.: *The Theory of Moral Hazard and Unobservable Behaviour. Part I*. Mimeo. Oxford: Nuffield College, Oxford University, 1975.

MLČOCH, L.: Chování československého podnikového sektoru [Behavior of the Czechoslovak Business Sector]. *VP* No. 384. Praha: Ekonomický ústav ČSAV, 1990.

MLČOCH, L.: Privatizace bez kapitálu [Privatization without Capital]. *Finance a úvěr* 54, 11–12 (2004): 560–63.

MLČOCH, L.: *Ekonomie důvěry a společného dobra* [Economics of Confidence and Common Good]. Praha: Karolinum. 2006.

MOSTELLER, F., NOGEE, P.: An Experimental Measurement of Utility. *Journal of Political Economy* 59, 5 (1951): 371–404.

NEUMANN, J. VON, MORGENSTERN, O.: *Theory of Games and Economic Behavior*. 3rd ed. Princeton: Princeton University Press, 1953.

NEWBERY, D. M. G., STIGLITZ, J. E.: *The Theory of Commodity Price Stabilization: A Study in the Economics of Risk*. Oxford: Oxford University Press, 1981.

OLSON, M.: *The Logic of Collective Action. Public Goods and the Theory of Groups*. Cambridge, MA: Harvard University Press, 1965.

POLINSKY, A. M., SHAVELL, S.: The Economic Theory of Public Enforcement of Law. *Journal of Economic Literature* 38, 1 (2000): 45–76.

PRESTON, M. G., BARATTA, P.: An Experimental Study of the Auction-Value of an Uncertain Outcome. *American Journal of Psychology* 61, 2 (1948): 183–93.

RANAWEERA, T.: Foreign Aid, Conditionality and Ghost of the Financing Gap: A Forgotten Aspect of the Aid Debate. *World Bank Policy Research Paper* No. 3019, World Bank, 2003.

REICHLOVÁ, N., CAHLÍK, T., HLAVÁČEK, J., ŠVARC, P.: Multiagent Approaches in Economics. In *Mathematical Methods in Economics*, edited by L. Lukáš, 77–98. Plzeň: Západočeská univerzita, 2006.

ROSS, A.: The Economic Theory of Agency: The Principal's Problems. *American Economic Review* 63, 2 (1973): 134–39.

ROTHSCHILD, M., STIGLITZ, J. E.: Equilibrium in Competitive Insurance Markets: An Essay on the Economics of Imperfect Information. *Quarterly Journal of Economics* 90, 4 (1976): 629–49.

SACHS, J.: Conditionality, Debt Relief, and the Developing Country Debt Crisis. In *Developing Country Debt and World Economy*, edited by J. Sachs, 275–84. Chicago: University of Chicago Press, 1989.

SEN, A.: *On Ethics and Economics*. Oxford: Blackwell, 1987.

SIMON, H. A.: Theories of Bounded Rationality. In *Decision and Organization*, edited by C. B. McGuire, R. Radner, 161–76. Amsterdam: North Holland, 1972.

SIMON, H. A.: A Mechanism for Social Selection and Successful Altruism. *Science* 250, 4988 (1990): 1665–68.

SKOŘEPA, M.: Daniel Kahneman a psychologické základy ekonomie [Daniel Kahneman and basic psychological principles of economics]. *Politická ekonomie* 52, 2 (2004): 247–55.

SKOŘEPA, M.: Zpochybnění deskriptivnosti teorie očekávaného užitku [Impeachment of the descriptive character of the theory of expected utility]. *WP IES* No. 7. Praha: Fakulta sociálních věd UK, 2006.

SMITH, A.: *The Theory of Moral Sentiments*. New Rochelle, NY: Arlington House, 1969.

SPULBER, D. F.: *Market Microstructure: Intermediaries and the Theory of the Firm*. Cambridge: Cambridge University Press, 1999.

STIGLITZ, J.: Incentives, Risk and Information: Notes Toward a Theory of Hierarchy. *Bell Journal of Economics* 6, 2 (1975): 552–79.

SVENSSON, J.: When Is Foreign Aid Policy Credible? Aid Dependence and Conditionality. *Journal of Development Economics* 61, 1 (2000): 61–84.

THALER, R. H.: Mental Accounting and Consumer Choice. *Marketing Science* 4, 3 (1985): 199–214.

TIEBOUT, C.: The Pure Theory of Local Expenditure. *Journal of Political Economy* 64, 5 (1956): 416–24.

TURNOVEC, F.: Who Are the Principals and Who Are the Agents? A Leontief-type Model of Ownership Structures. *Finance a úvěr* 50, 11 (2000): 648–50.

TVERSKY, A.: Intransitivity of Preferences. *Psychological Review* 76, 1 (1969): 31–48.

TVERSKY, A., KAHNEMAN, D.: Judgment under Uncertainty: Heuristics and Biases. *Science* 185, 4157 (1974): 1124–31.

TVERSKY, A., KAHNEMAN, D.: The Framing of Decisions and the Psychology of Choice. *Science* 211, 4481 (1981): 453–58.

VANEK, J.: *The General Theory of Labor-Managed Market Economies*. Ithaca: Cornell University Press, 1970.

VARIAN, H. R.: *Microeconomic Analysis*. 3rd ed. New York: W. W. Norton, 1992.

VEBLEN, T.: *The Theory of the Leisure Class: An Economic Study of Institutions*. New York: Macmillan, 1899.

VIVES, X., ED.: *Corporate Governance: Theoretical and Empirical Perspectives*. Cambridge: Cambridge University Press, 2000.

WARD, B.: *The Socialist Economy*. New York: Random House, 1967.

WILSON, E. O.: *On Human Nature*. Cambridge: Harvard University Press, 1978.

ZIELENIEC, J. ET AL.: *Československo na rozcestí* [Czechoslovakia on the Cross-road]. Praha: Lidové noviny, 1990.

NAME INDEX

GENERALIZED
MICROECONOMICS

JIŘÍ HLAVÁČEK AND MICHAL HLAVÁČEK

ENGLISH TRANSLATION BY SIMON VOLLAM
PUBLISHED BY CHARLES UNIVERSITY IN PRAGUE
KAROLINUM PRESS
OVOCNÝ TRH 3–5, 116 36 PRAGUE 1, CZECH REPUBLIC
(CUPRESS.CUNI.CZ)
PRAGUE 2013

EDITED BY JAN HAVLÍČEK
LAYOUT AND COVER DESIGN JAN ŠERÝCH
TYPESET BY STUDIO LACERTA (WWW.SAZBA.CZ)
PRINTED BY KAROLINUM PRESS
FIRST ENGLISH EDITION
ISBN 978-80-246-2024-4